Smart Marketing for Associations

Marketing Plans that Work

By M. Michelle Poskaitis

asae | american society of association executives

Washington, DC

Information in this book is accurate as of the time of publication and consistent with standards of good practice in the general management community. As research and practice advance, however, standards may change. For this reason, it is recommended that readers evaluate the applicability of any recommendation in light of particular situations and changing standards.

American Society of Association Executives
1575 I Street, NW
Washington, DC 20005-1103
Phone: (888) 950-2723
Fax: (202) 408-9634
E-mail: books@asaenet.org

ASAE's core purpose is to advance the value of voluntary associations to society and to support the professionalism of the individuals who lead them.

Susan Robertson, Vice President, Marketing and Communications
Anna Nunan, Director of Book Publishing
Louise Quinn, Acquisitions Coordinator
Jennifer Moon, Production Manager
Anthony Conley, Operations Coordinator
Edited by Katherine L. George, ABC, CAE

Cover design by Deborah Dutton & Joseph Sherman Design and interior design by Black Dot

This book is available at a special discount when ordered in bulk quantities. For information, contact the ASAE Member Service Center at (202) 371-0940.

A complete catalog of titles is available on the ASAE Web site at www.asaenet.org/bookstore

For O

Contents

— continued on following page

Contents

List of Tables

— continued on following page

List of Tables

Foreword

Time and attention. That's what we are all competing for—the time and attention of our members and customers, sponsors and advertisers, senior management and staff. The competition is fierce and technology geometrically increases the challenge, crippling our ability to lead, to manage, and to achieve the mission.

So how do you attract attention and engage stakeholders? How do you stay focused on what really matters and avoid endless distractions? Goal-oriented people know that if you write it down, you can make it happen. A written marketing plan can go a long way toward keeping your entire association moving.

In *Smart Marketing for Associations: Marketing Plans that Work*, Michelle Poskaitis has crafted a simple, effective, how-to guide for association executives that makes it easy to adapt the logic and methodology of commercial marketing planning to the unique challenge of advancing a mission, cause, profession or industry.

The marketing planning process can create marketing champions at every level of the association, integrating action across department lines. Written marketing plans capture all the assumptions, goals, agreements, ideas, deadlines, and assignments that provide an annual benchmark for continuous improvement.

Although strategic planning provides direction and budget planning details revenue and expense assumptions, there is a wide gap between vision and reality. Strategic marketing can close that gap, creating the products, services, programs, initiatives, events, and experiences—all of the transactions and interactions with those you serve. Marketing plans can create a shared reality of what it will take to make it happen.

As the chief marketing officer (CMO), the association executive is responsible for integrating every aspect of the association into a coherent whole, aligning staff and volunteer activities with the vision and mission of the organization.

The marketing plan is the communication tool, the sheet music, which can mobilize an extended network of supporters and allies, synthesizing countless ideas and actions into one powerful movement.

The marketing plan is also your best hope at overcoming "Knowledge Age ADS," the new attention deficit syndrome that afflicts customers and staff alike. The CMO can provide clarity, direction and focus; marketing professionals—outsourced or on staff—can provide the tools and techniques.

Smart Marketing for Associations: Marketing Plans that Work is a comprehensive outline for marketing planning, but don't be intimidated by the analytical requirements. Start small. Attack a single product launch or build on promotion plans already in place. Just do it. Marketing planning is as much a habit as a skill, so the sooner you start, the better off you will be a year from now.

Marketing planning is not a theoretical exercise, and cannot be done in a vacuum. Get out there. Find and develop marketing champions throughout the organization, among staff and volunteer leadership.

After all, marketing is not a department—it's a perspective. Use marketing to help unite people with a quest. Use marketing plans to communicate each individual's role. Infuse the mission and vision with passion and go change the world.

Ann Oliveri, CAE

Senior Vice President, Strategic Development
ULI—The Urban Land Institute
Washington, DC

Preface

This text was inspired by my participation on the American Society of Association Executives (ASAE) Marketing Section Council in its effort to articulate a core competency standard for association marketing. The council is comprised of volunteer leaders of the ASAE Marketing Section, a professional membership network within ASAE consisting of more than 5,000 association marketers and executives nationwide. Their common denominator is hands-on expertise and sustained success in association marketing.

In 2000, one key goal was to identify the essential business concepts, practices, and skills association marketers need to be successful in their jobs. The resulting association marketing core competencies (shown in Appendix 1) include these eight domains of practice: marketing planning, market research, customer strategy, product and service strategy, distribution strategy, pricing strategy, marketing communications, and business management.

The focus of this text is on how to develop a strategic marketing plan. In the process of learning to do it, you'll pick up practical knowledge about all the other marketing principles as well. Some people imagine there's a secret code to unlock the mystery of successful marketing plans—that perhaps there's some business know-how or writing style they'll possess only after acquiring an MBA or CAE. Those are useful credentials but not necessary ones. In strategic marketing planning, asking the right questions can be as challenging as finding the answers. We've already done that thinking for you. You'll learn the definitions of key terms, considerations, and calculation formulas to quantify, substantiate, and present a professional marketing plan.

In my view, strategic marketing is both art and science, creative and logical. My goal is to educate and empower you in the art and science of strategic marketing planning. Enjoy!

M. Michelle Poskaitis

Acknowledgments

To my dear friend and the world's best executive coach, **Rick Wright,** President, Simple Spirit, Inc., Santa Monica, California, thank you for always being there with clarity, inspiration, and care.

My deep appreciation belongs to those who generously shared their marketing wisdom and personal encouragement to help me complete this book. To **Steve Baker,** CEO, National Association of Intercollegiate Athletics, Kansas City, Missouri, thanks for being an extraordinary entrepreneur in the nonprofit world. To **Daniell T. Griffin,** Director, Direct Response & Publication Marketing, Epilepsy Foundation of America, Upper Marlboro, Maryland, and member of the board of directors, Direct Marketing Association of Washington, D.C., thank you for sharing the journey through life's challenges and triumphs—and all the transformations we've yet to experience together. To **John Gunn,** CEO, John Gunn Marketing Partners, Arlington, Virginia, my *compadre* in freedom—thank you for sharing your marketing genius.

To **Stephen P. Hines,** Principal, Marketing Resource Management, Aldie, Virginia, and Executive Director, E.S.Africa.com, Middleburg, Virginia, your loyalty and friendship are beyond measure—and far greater than even that bizarre sense of humor and knack for soliloquy. To **Maura Kiey,** former Vice President of Marketing, The Outsourcing Institute, Long Island, New York, your uncanny sensibilities are always appreciated. Thank you for sharing your insight with humor. To **Ann Oliveri,** Senior Vice President, Strategic Development, ULI—Urban Land Institute, Washington, D.C.—a true change agent—your willingness to turn things upside down always inspires me.

To **Inger Wilson,** Owner, Studio.i Graphics, Herndon, Virginia, thank you for your uncanny ability to ask the right questions and for having the heart to care about the answers. To **Richard Yep,** Executive Director, American Counseling Association, Alexandria, Virginia, thank you for your business creativity, unparalleled diplomacy, and most of all, your gentle honesty. To **Michelle Zinnert,** Marketing Director, American Association of Blood Banks, Bethesda, Maryland, and Vice Chair, ASAE Marketing Section Council, thank you for your enthusiasm and commitment to make a difference.

About the Author
M. Michelle Poskaitis

M. Michelle Poskaitis is CEO of Originations Marketing LLC in Falls Church, Virginia. She is an author and strategic marketing communication consultant specializing in marketing strategy, planning, and integrated communications for associations, nonprofits, and small businesses. Clients include professional societies, trade associations, and philanthropic organizations as well as marketing agencies and other entrepreneurial corporations.

Michelle is the 2001–2002 chair of the ASAE Marketing Council, a professional membership network of more than 5,000 association marketers and executives worldwide. She is editor of *Executive IdeaLink, Marketing Fast Facts,* and *Communication News,* monthly online newsletters published by ASAE; and a contributor to such magazines as *Executive Update* and *National Public Accountant.*

Michelle was profiled in *Nation's Business* magazine article "Consultants to the Rescue," published by the U.S. Chamber of Commerce, and received the Professional News Media Association Award for excellence in publishing. A former news reporter, she was also employed as executive director of the U.S. Federation of Small Businesses and held senior staff positions with several Washington, D.C.–based associations.

The author welcomes and encourages your comments and feedback at (703)-379-5354 or mmp@originations.net.

Chapter 1

Engage Your Marketing Mind

Marketing Myopia:

Short-sightedness in marketing; a failure by an organization to define its mission enough, resulting in the over-emphasis of product and the under-emphasis of customer needs and wants.

— Don Bradmore, Marketing Professor

There's a basic logic to a strategic marketing plan and this book will guide you through every step. You'll learn the words, math, thinking process, and presentation formats to construct a viable marketing agenda for the next twelve months. Each chapter relates to a specific section of your marketing plan and contains key questions whose answers will form the basis of your narrative content. Best of all, this book will save you loads of time with its preformatted charts and tables for presenting quantitative data in a logical, consumable format. Along the way you'll gain a better understanding of association marketing principles and best practices.

What Is Strategic Marketing?

Before developing a marketing plan, it's important to understand strategic marketing. Strategic marketing is at once a business philosophy and a practical discipline of association management that pervades every function of the organization with a focus on the customer and the world in which they live. It requires clear understanding and articulation of the past and the present as well as your best guess about what might happen in the future. Strategic marketing is characteristically "outside-in" (versus "inside-out") in that your attention originates with the customer (versus the association), which ultimately helps you create products, services, and experiences to ensure an ongoing, satisfying relationship between the organization and the customer.

For decades the *four Ps* (product, price, place, and promotion) served as the framework for effective marketing management. The blend of these four variables resulted in the *marketing mix* to form the basis of an organization's marketing initiatives. In a nutshell, the four Ps are:

Product: products and services an organization produces and sells (because it can)

Price: the amount charged (to cover costs and make as much profit as possible)

Place: where the organization distributes products or services (because they are the easiest, cheapest places to do so)

Promotion: what the organization says about the product or service (to the masses whenever, wherever, and however they want)

The four Ps framework evolved in an age of consumerism characterized by the saying *caveat emptor*—let the buyer beware.

That was 1960. We're in the next century!

Today, organizations need to adopt the *four Cs* (customer, cost, convenience, and communication) in framing strategic marketing initiatives to achieve organizational objectives. Coined by Robert F. Lauterborn, coauthor of *The New Marketing Paradigm: Integrated Marketing Communications* (NTC Business Books, 1997), the four Cs encourage us to operate our organizations from the customer-versus-product perspective. Lauterborn's advice is:

Consumer: "Forget product. Study consumer wants and needs. You can no longer sell whatever you can make. You can only sell what someone specifically wants to buy.

Cost: "Forget price. Understand the consumers' cost to satisfy their want or need.

Convenience: "Forget place. Think convenience to buy.

Communication: "Finally, forget promotion. The word is *communication*."

Lauterborn's approach isn't a marketing fad. It's a fundamental shift in management philosophy and practice, primarily in response to dramatic changes in how people decide to purchase. So, while the product or service is an essential ingredient, it's pointless without a customer. Pricing impacts profits but only to the extent that the customer will buy at your price points. Therefore your pricing needs to consider cost recovery as well as the customer's intellectual, emotional, and sensate response to paying the sales price.

With the Internet and increased competition, availability of comparable products and services is infinite. How convenient do you make it for customers to acquire your products or services? Are the books and magazines you publish available at Amazon.com, the local Borders bookstore, at your annual meeting, and directly from your association?

Fifty years ago, mass marketing worked. Promotion focused on mass distribution of the same message. Since then, several generations of consumers have grown up in a culture pervaded with media. Remember, television didn't exist before the 1950s and the Internet was primarily used only by academics before 1975. Now old and young alike are inundated with advertising messages daily. Like any long-term relationship, two-way communication is essential. In today's economy it's too easy for customers to take their dollars elsewhere.

It's the twenty-first century! Today and tomorrow, associations need to truly be customer oriented versus product oriented.

The Marketing Mindset

Successful marketing is not a random phenomenon. People who consistently win aren't lucky; they make it happen. As a practical matter in addition to creative, strategic marketing requires you to be:

1. Analytical. You must find, face, and act on the facts and logical assumptions of the market environment, target audience, available budget, and a host of other opportunities, limitations, and resources that converge to form your association's present reality. You'll also need to experiment and embrace the lessons learned from every success and failure.

2. Collaborative. Marketing is an integrated business discipline that directly impacts and requires input from every functional area of your association. You literally can't do effective marketing alone. Whether your association operates a centralized or decentralized marketing department or none at all, those responsible for the marketing function (and this text assumes that's you) need the wisdom, resources, and cooperation of all stakeholders, especially coworkers, service providers, strategic partners, customers, and others, to accomplish the association's goals. Collaboration and open communication ensures credibility with and buy-in from your colleagues.

3. Curious. Effective marketing requires a wholesome, eager desire to learn and be informed—by our customers, competitors, market opportunities, new strategies, successes, and failures. It asks you to consistently strive for a

360-degree view of a moving target; to observe as an enthusiast in the bleachers, a coach along the sidelines, a player on the bench, a reporter in the media box, a fan tuning in for the play by play, and a team player who scores the winning goal.

4. Flexible. As markets evolve you need to meet your customers where they are. As products and services age you need to redesign, repackage, or retire. When operations break down you need to adjust people and priorities. You need to bend—and even contort—without breaking. Sometimes that means going with the flow. Sometimes that means interrupting and redirecting the flow. Other times that means turning a program upside down for a new perspective. However you and your organization choose to achieve it, flexibility is essential.

5. Committed. It takes time and constancy to nurture and sustain profitable relationships with prospects and customers. Big goals require sustained, collaborative action over time, and most strategic marketing initiatives need more than twelve months to mature and be fully productive. You need to think and act in the long term while achieving short-term milestones that consistently move the organization toward a desired future.

Follow the advice in this text and you'll engage a marketing mindset for yourself.

What Is a Marketing Plan?

A marketing plan examines internal and external conditions and articulates *how* and *why* who is doing *what* by *when* for the customer. It's a map that shows you where you are, identifies where you want to go, and charts a course to arrive on time within budget. More important, the process of developing a marketing plan requires you to investigate, answer, and communicate several issues comprehensively, including:

- Who are our customers? Why?

- What do our customers want and need? Why?

- What are the current market dynamics and trends?

- What are our business objectives? Why?

- What advantages and challenges do we face in achieving the objectives?

- How will we achieve the objectives?

- How will the actions we take this year support the association's strategic plan and goals?

- What are we selling? Why?

- How will we position and communicate our products and services in the market?

- Who will take what specific actions by when?

- How much will necessary resources cost?

Often the term *marketing plan* is used to refer to nothing more than a glorified list of promotional tactics. Promotion is only one aspect of marketing. Although related tactics contained within a marketing plan will be discussed here, they equate to one chapter in a far grander story. A marketing plan is a natural outgrowth of an organization's strategic plan. If your association doesn't have a formal strategic plan, at a minimum the association's mission and vision statements govern and provide boundaries to ensure your marketing plan is aligned with the overall purpose of your organization.

A marketing plan is a written, actionable document—not a concept, thought, or great idea tossed around in a meeting. It simply doesn't count unless you write it down and implement it. There are many formats and styles for marketing plans, depending on how the organization intends to use one. For example, a marketing plan presented to potential investors is typically shorter and more concise, with a bit more persuasive spin, than a marketing plan intended as a working document to be used by day-to-day managers. Here we'll outline the aspects most common to successful marketing plans and provide easy, timesaving tools to present quantitative data. A sample outline showing the basic structure of a marketing plan appears at the end of this chapter.

An effective marketing plan is also an ending and a beginning. It is a summation of research, analysis, and collaborative strategic decision making, but it's only a starting point for implementation. This text will walk you through each step of data collection, relational thinking exercises, strategy development, and results measurements to build a successful marketing plan.

Keep in mind that once you set forth strategies and tactics, markets will change and breakdowns will inevitably occur. While the marketing plan provides a fundamental baseline, it's not static. You need to review the plan periodically and adjust as you gain more information about and experience with your target audience. That's not a green light to avoid accountability. Rather, as you implement the plan you will discover information that, if it had been available in the planning process, would have changed your approach. The marketing plan should clearly define present circumstances and future goals while allowing some flexibility in how you reach the goals.

Benefits for Your Association

Developing a marketing plan for your organization can gobble up limited resources (time, people, money) and isn't valuable unless it's implemented. So why bother? Good question. Some of the benefits you gain include:

Saving money. A balance of planning and implementation ultimately serves the association's profitability. An absence of a marketing plan can actually cost you more than you're currently spending on marketing. Many nonprofit organizations invest too little time in marketing planning, leaving themselves with little more than "blame, shame, and guilt" to account for a lack of desired results. Conversely, spending too much time planning without taking action to implement is also costly.

Common focus. Imagine a scenario in which the meeting planner is negotiating and creating logistics for a 2,000-person conference and the marketing manager is developing promotions to register 500 attendees. A disaster waiting to happen. Each element of a marketing plan tempers every other element, providing a context within which everyone in the organization collaborates to develop assumptions, projections, and planned initiatives. So while in theory one colleague projects revenue from the sale of 5,000 books, if the organization has the budget to produce only 3,000, staff must negotiate to either adjust the sales goal, expense budget, or production schedule. Marketing planning allows your organization to establish clear, unified market assumptions and forecasts that focus everyone's effort on achieving the same goal.

Increased agility. Marketing planning gives your organization a logical process to channel what you know and what you assume into a consumable tool the entire organization can use. It encourages you to question current assumptions and test new ones. The process ultimately hones your ability to move the organization forward, because you are clear about where you are, where you want to be, and what hurdles (and help) are in between. As a result, you're in a much better position to act on unexpected opportunities, respond to unforeseen changes, and ultimately achieve goals.

Performance measurement. How do you, your boss, or the board of directors define success? A marketing plan clearly defines success and gives you much of the information you need to be successful in your job. It serves as a rudder to help you set priorities, organize and manage resources, make decisions, and operate effectively.

Competitive advantage. Think your for-profit competitors are leaving marketing success to chance? Not a chance! Neither should you. Some might argue that nonprofit organizations are inherently different from for-profit corporations and may, therefore, be managed with less rigor or formality. Let's assume that's true. Developing a marketing plan actually allows (and demands) that your organization identify and leverage all of its uniqueness most effectively and thereby fund achievement of its mission.

Marketing Plan Structure and Evolution

The first attempt at developing a strategic marketing plan can appear to be a daunting task. It does require a lot of thinking, communication, time, and effort. This book will ease the process by helping you build each section of the plan in logical sequence. The good news is that once you've established the plan structure, as well as controls and measurements to generate supporting data, the process becomes easier year after year and your plan grows more comprehensive and useful. A strategic marketing plan truly is an ever-evolving document and your first is typically the worst. If you're starting from scratch, develop as much of the plan as possible now and include initiatives in the next twelve months that will help you refine the planning process next year. Let's get started.

Strategic Marketing Plan Outline

Here's what the table of contents in your marketing plan will look like when you've progressed through this entire book:

I.   EXECUTIVE SUMMARY
    A. Introduction
    B. Overview of Situation Analysis
    C. Overview of Products and Services
    D. Summary of Objectives
    E. Overview of Positioning and Key Strategies
    F. Summary of Resource Requirements

II. SITUATION ANALYSIS
    A. Market Environment
       1. Market Profile

         2. Market Universe, Market Share and Growth, Supply and Demand
         3. Market Dynamics and Trends
         4. Competition and Pricing
     B. Association Environment
         1. Customer Profile
         2. SWOT Analysis
         3. Product and Service Information
            a. Description
            b. Features, Advantages, Benefits
            c. Pricing, Sales, and Revenue Trends

III.   FORECASTS
     A. Summary of Key Issues
     B. Market Forecasts
     C. Sales Forecasts

IV.   OBJECTIVES
     A. Business Objectives
     B. Marketing Objectives

V.   POSITIONING

VI.   STRATEGIES AND TACTICS

VII.   RESOURCE REQUIREMENTS
     A. Staffing
     B. Timing
     C. Information Needs
     D. Budget

VIII.   CONTROLS AND MEASUREMENTS

Chapter 2

Understand the Market

To know oneself is wisdom,
but to know one's neighbor is genius.

—Norman Douglas, Novelist

The Situation Analysis

Your *situation analysis* is an examination of the significant circumstances and conditions of your internal and external environments, to understand their nature, proportion, function, and interrelationships. The information you glean and report in the situation analysis forms the basis of the remainder of your marketing plan—and every marketing decision you'll make. It should be an ongoing information gathering process as much as it is an essential section of your marketing plan.

Be highly curious at this stage of marketing planning. Imagine yourself an investigative news reporter looking for the untold story—or a detective seeking clues to the truth. Set your opinions and assumptions free and rely instead on substantiated evidence (aka primary and secondary market research) to define both the harsh and pleasant realities your association faces.

Format

Situation analyses are generally presented in narrative form, sprinkled with charts and graphs to summarize comparative data where appropriate. Start with an examination of the external environment (the market), followed by your internal environment (your association).

Market Research and Profile

Your *market* is the sum of all customers and potential customers (whether individuals or organizations) who want or need your products or services—and can afford them. A *market segment* is a subset of the market with like characteristics whose wants, needs, and purchasing habits are similar. *Market segmentation* is the practice of dividing the market into smaller groups sharing similar characteristics.

Defining your market is accomplished through *market research*—the collection, analysis, interpretation, and reporting of quantitative and qualitative information for marketing decision making. There are two main sources of market research information. *Primary market research* is information gathering conducted by your organization, either in house or by commissioning a research firm. *Secondary market research* is information collected and published by outside organizations such as industry experts, government agencies, academic institutions, other associations, and the media.

Primary Market Research

Your direct observation of and interaction with customers and prospects is very important. You must be responsible for knowing your customers and target audiences. Consumer retail marketers sit in shopping malls to observe customer behavior. You can do that at your annual meeting. Watch the traffic flow, see how members interact with products in the bookstore, and sit in on education sessions to observe the customer experience. Interact directly with customers and get to know them. Doing so creates invaluable institutional knowledge that can be confirmed with market research.

There are three basic information collection methods for primary market research: *focus groups*, which are facilitated face-to-face discussions among a small group representing the market; *surveys*, that is, questionnaires sent via mail or e-mail; and *informational interviews*, those one-on-one question-and-answer conversations typically conducted via telephone.

Market research encompasses the collection of four types of information, all based on customer characteristics.

1. *Demographic information* distinguishes a range of physical, social, and economic attributes such as age, gender, income level, marital status, and ethnic origin.

2. *Psychographic information* defines attitudes, beliefs, opinions, personalities, and lifestyles.

3. *Geographic information* identifies physical location—from country, state, region, and locale all the way down to exact street address.

4. *Behavioral information* offers insights into a customer's relationship to a specific type of product, service, or brand, factoring in desired benefits, usage, loyalty, and readiness to buy.

Full-blown market research is a highly complex discipline within strategic marketing. In simple terms, the process of knowing and understanding your marketing is rather like dating before committing to a relationship (see Table 2.1). On the first few dates, we get to know someone in conversation and other social interactions. At first blush we seek the "vital stats" about that person's life to eliminate any obvious compatibility obstacles. (Where are you from? Ever been married? Have any children? Where do you live? Where did you go to school? What do you do for fun? What did you think of that movie? Read any good books lately?)

In market research, conversations and social interactions equate to primary market research (focus groups, surveys, and interviews). The vital stats include demographic, geographic, and some psychographic information.

Let's continue with this analogy. Imagine you decide to spend more time together, and six months later that person is pushing commitment. You're not as certain, so you agree to attend the family reunion for an up-close-and-personal welcome to your date's world. As the day unfolds you realize that "annoying little habit" is actually a family pastime. And this person's primary role models for an intimate, committed relationship (the parents) leave you wondering whether your date is seeking a life partner or a caretaker.

In market research we'd call that collection of behavioral information regarding the person's desire (needs and motivations), experience and ability (usage), willingness (loyalty), and readiness to commit to (purchase) an *exclusive relationship* (product or service) with you (brand).

Secondary Market Research

Conducting secondary market research would be like reading about your date in the newspaper or yearbook—information that somebody else collected and published. You're never sure about the methodology, and it's not as intuitive or in-depth as personal experience, though it will generate interesting clues and perhaps a few eye-openers.

Table 2.1 Market Research: Akin to Dating	
Market Research	**Dating: Tell me about yourself**
Collected via focus groups, surveys, and interviews	Occurs via conversations
Demographic	
Age	"I'm 34 years old, graduated from XYU, and work as a manager at ABC Co.
Occupation	
Income	"I just got a promotion and finally hit six figures! I'm single, never married, no children, and live with one roommate in a town-house in Northern Virginia—the Old Town section of Alexandria.
Marital status	
Family size	
Household size	
Geographic	
Psychographic	
Attitudes	"I love learning about different cultures and always vacation abroad.
Beliefs	"I think traveling makes a person well rounded and interesting, though I often find the airlines uncooperative. I'm a firstborn over-achiever and hope to raise a family one day.
Personality	
Lifestyle	
Behavioral	
Desired benefit(s)	"Right now I really want to buy a luxury car. I own a Toyota Corolla but it's on its last legs and too small for such a long daily commute to the office. I like Toyotas but am leaning toward a Mercedes or a BMW and will likely buy next month."
User status	
Usage rate	
Loyalty status	
Buyer readiness	

Format

Once this information has been collected, you may choose to convey it in narrative or chart form. For complex markets or multiple customer segments, a "market profile sheet" (see Table 2) helps organize key information. Choose a combination that allows you to convey maximum information in minimum space.

Table 2.2 Market Profile Sheet	Market Segment 1	Market Segment 2	Market Segment 3
Demographics			
Gender, age range			
Median income			
Highest degree achieved			
Marital status			
Professional title			
Other characteristics			
Geographics			
Country			
State/region			
Locale			
Psychographics			
Attitudes			
Beliefs			
Opinions			
Personality			
Lifestyle			
Behaviorals			
Desired benefits/motivations			
Product/service user status			
Rate/frequency of product/service use			
Degree of loyalty			
Repeat purchaser?			
Readiness to buy			

Note: State the source of the information: month, year, and name of proprietary or published references.

Market Universe, Share, Growth, Supply, and Demand

Once you identify the market profile information, you'll need to understand and articulate the size and nature of the market. So first, let's review key terms commonly used to define the market environment and your association's participation in that environment.

Market universe, also known as *market potential*, is the totality of the market expressed in size or dollar value (*i.e.*, all customers and potential customers who want or need your products and services, can afford them, and are expected to buy them).

Market share is the percentage of the market that currently buys a specific product or service from your organization compared to your competitors'. Market share is expressed as a percentage of the total number of customers and a percentage of the dollar value of total sales for the entire market. Typically it is measured annually.

Market growth rate, also known as *compound annual growth rate (CAGR)*, is the degree by which a market is increasing or decreasing in size, expressed as a percentage per year.

Supply is the amount of a product or service type that is available for purchase at a given price.

Demand refers to the volume or extent of the market's customers that are ready and able to buy your product or service at a certain price.

Formula

To develop this next section of the situation analysis, address the following questions and study the formulas shown in the tables that immediately follow:

- What is the market universe today compared to the last three to five years?

- What is our market share today compared to the last three to five years?

- What is the current market growth rate compared to the last three to five years?

- What is the current product or service supply compared to the past three to five years?

- What is the current product or service demand compared to the past three to five years?

- What clearly defined segments exist within the market?

- How are those segments defined and characterized?

- How are market segments dependent or not dependent on products or services?

- What terminology, performance indicators, and measures are unique to this market?

Format

Much of this information will be presented in narrative form, substantiated by key summary charts. Study Tables 2.3–2.7. Be sure to cite all references to data including internal association reports.

Market Dynamics and Trends

To understand your market you will also need to examine the overarching economic, social, legal, political, and technological forces that impact the market and thereby influence customer purchasing behavior.

Definitions

Market dynamics are uncontrollable external variables that impact your association's ability to generate sales. *Market trends* address previous and anticipated tendencies in relation to the current market situation. Your attention to these factors is essential to spot and exploit new market opportunities and for other ongoing marketing decision making.

Demographic trends include the size, location, age, ethnicity, gender, occupation, and other aspects of the population. *Economic trends* like interest rates, current cost of living, per capita income, and discretionary income are variables that directly impact consumer spending. *Technology trends* include factors that drive the invention of new technologies and subsequent acceptance and use by consumers. *Social trends* address cultural values, practices, ethics, and points of view. *Political trends* include legal and regulatory affairs as well as public interest initiatives.

Much of the information about market dynamics and trends will come from secondary market research sources such as government agencies, academic institutions, other associations, and the media as well as your instincts. It's a good practice to save pertinent articles and studies you find throughout the year to compile this section of next year's marketing plan.

Table 2.3   Market Share Trend Analysis by Product or Service Type

	2002	2001	2000	1999	Gain/Loss Over Last Year	Gain/Loss 1999 to 2002
Product/Service Type 1						
Your Association Product/Service Trade Name	39%	46.5%	41%	25%	27.5%	+14%
Competitor 1 Product/Service Trade Name	45%	39.5%	37%	38%	+5.5%	+7%
Competitor 2 Product/Service Trade Name	11%	8.6%	17%	31%	+2.4%	−20%
Total Product/Service Type 1	100%	100%	100%	100%		
Product/Service Type 2						
Your Association Product/Service Trade Name	%	%	%	%	+/−%	+/−%
Competitor 1 Product/Service Trade Name	%	%	%	%	+/−%	+/−%
Competitor 2 Product/Service Trade Name	%	%	%	%	+/−%	+/−%
Competitor 3 Product/Service Trade Name	%	%	%	%	+/−%	+/−%
Competitor 4 Product/Service Trade Name	%	%	%	%	+/−%	+/−%
Total Product/Service Type 2	100%	100%	100%	100%		
Product/Service Type 3						
Your Association Product/Service Trade Name	%	%	%	%	+/−%	+/−%
Competitor 1 Product/Service Trade Name	%	%	%	%	+/−%	+/−%
Competitor 2 Product/Service Trade Name	%	%	%	%	+/−%	+/−%
Competitor 3	%	%	%	%	+/−%	+/−%
Product/Service Trade Name						
Total Product/Service Type 3	100%	100%	100%	100%		
Total Share All Product and Service Types	%	%	%	%		

Note: State the source of the information: month, year, and name of proprietary or published references.

16

Table 2.4 Market Share Trend Analysis by Market Segment						
	2002	2001	2000	1999	Gain/Loss Over Last Year	Gain/Loss 1999 to 2002
Market Segment 1						
Your Association Product/Service Trade Name	%	%	%	%	+/−%	+/−%
Competitor 1 Product/Service Trade Name	%	%	%	%	+/−%	+/−%
Competitor 2 Product/Service Trade Name	%	%	%	%	+/−%	+/−%
Market Segment 2						
Your Association Product/Service Trade Name	%	%	%	%	+/−%	+/−%
Competitor 1 Product/Service Trade Name	%	%	%	%	+/−%	+/−%
Competitor 2 Product/Service Trade Name	%	%	%	%	+/−%	+/−%
Market Segment 3						
Your Association Product/Service Trade Name	%	%	%	%	+/−%	+/−%
Competitor 1 Product/Service Trade Name	%	%	%	%	+/−%	+/−%
Competitor 2 Product/Service Trade Name	%	%	%	%	+/−%	+/−%
Total Share All Segments	%	%	%	%	+/−%	+/−%

Note: State the source of the information: month, year, and name of proprietary or published references.

Table 2.5	Market Supply by Product or Service Type	
Year	**Dollar Value**	**Volume**
	All units produced by each competitor × Avg. sales price of each competitor added together = Dollar value of market supply	All units produced by each competitor added together = Unit volume of market supply
2004	$	#
2003	$	#
2002	$	#
2001	$	#

Note: State the source of the information: month, year, and name of proprietary or published references.

Table 2.6	Market Demand by Product or Service Type	
Year	**Dollar Value** Total dollar value of all unit sales by all competitors	**Volume** Total number of units sold by all competitors
2004	$	#
2003	$	#
2002	$	#
200	$	#

Note: State the source of the information: month, year, and name of proprietary or published references.

Year	Dollar Value (thousands)	Growth Rate	Volume	Growth Rate (units)
		Dollar value of most recent year — Dollar value of immediate prior year ÷ Dollar value of immediate prior year × 100 = %		Number of product/service units of most recent year — Number of product/service units of immediate prior year ÷ Number of product/ service of immediate prioryear × 100 = %
2005	$500	+20%	2000	+20%
2004	$415	−14%	1500	−22%
2003	$485	+/−%	1940	+/−%
2002		+/−%		+/−%
Avg.				

Table 2.7   Market Growth Rate by Product or Service Type

Note 1: State the source of the information: month, year, and name of proprietary or published references.

Note 2: If the dollar value of the most recent year is greater than the immediate prior year, the growth rate is a percentage increase; if less, it is a percentage decrease. Similarly, if the number of units of the most recent year is greater than the number of units of the immediate prior year, the growth rate is a percentage increase; if less, a percentage decrease.

Formula

In this section of the situation analysis, address these questions:

- Why does this market exist?

- How long has this market existed?

- What caused this market to form? What forces cause the market to be sustained?

- How did the market evolve, change, or develop in the past 10 years? In the past three years?

- Is the market growing, static, or shrinking? In what ways? Why?

- What market characteristics are new, interesting, surprising, or odd?

- How does the international marketplace differ from the domestic marketplace?

- What factors influence or affect the target audiences? How?

- How rapidly is change occurring?

- What economic, political, cultural, and technological factors affect the market?

- What legislative or regulatory actions influence market dynamics? How?

- What do market experts, analysts, and the media report?

- What new or alternative products or services influence customer behavior?

Format

This information is typically presented in narrative form, substantiated by references to third-party reports, articles, and other information.

Competition and Pricing
Definitions

Competitors are organizations that vie for the same market. Competitors come in all shapes and sizes. A competitor could be an organization similar to yours, seeking the same customer segments by offering the same products or services. Or competitors could be organizations offering different versions of the same basic product or service type. Competitors could also be organizations that offer completely different products or services that satisfy the wants and needs of the same customers as yours.

A *competitive analysis* examines and reports a range of information about your competitors for comparison with your organization. That information typically is gleaned piecemeal through a variety of third-party experts and other public information. A good resource for learning how to collect competitor information is the Society of Competitive Intelligence Professionals, www.scip.org. Points of comparison unique to your industry and market generally include the following:

- Organization type and size

- Market longevity

- Goals and strategies

- Range and quality of product and service offerings

- Cost to produce and sell

- Product and service pricing

- Market segments served (by customer type, geography, and so on)
- Market position and share
- Marketing channels
- Resources and capabilities
- Strengths, weaknesses, opportunities, and threats (SWOT)

The value of a competitive analysis is to understand each competitor's *competitive position*—its ranking in the market relative to your association and other competitors—as well as each competitor's *market advantage*, the primary benefit that satisfies customer wants and needs more effectively than a competitor's.

Once complete, a comparative analysis of competitors makes it easy to spot significant differentials, which helps you discern your advantages and weaknesses in the market and spot potential market allies. Understanding your place in the market today is essential to set realistic goals, develop relevant positioning and strategies, and benchmark marketing performance.

Formula

Start by collecting public information about each competitor: its products, services, and pricing. Your ability to collect competitor information will vary. If you're competing with a publicly traded company, lots of information is available. However, more often than not, associations compete with other associations and private for-profit corporations that guard proprietary information.

One way to learn about competitors is to become their prospect or customer. Other general sources of competitor information will come from secondary market research sources as well as direct interaction at trade expositions, conferences, and other market events. It's also a good practice to collect and save trade press articles as well as competitor's marketing, advertising, and public relations materials throughout the year to compile this section of next year's marketing plan.

To guide your investigation and analysis of competitors, focus on information to complete the Competitor Matrix, Competitor Product and Service Matrix, and Competitive Pricing Analysis shown in Tables 2.8–2.10.

Next, as best as possible, conduct an analysis of each competitor's strengths, weaknesses, opportunities, and threats, known as a SWOT analysis. The next chapter discusses how to conduct a SWOT analysis of your association. The same formula applies to your competition.

In the competition and pricing section of the situation analysis, address the following questions:

- Who are the top five competitors?

- How does each competitor compete with your association? (product or service similarity, organization similarity, satisfaction of the same customer wants or needs)

- What products and services do competitors sell? (by product type and trade name)

- In what product categories do competitors compete directly with your association?

- What is the available supply of direct competitors? (by product or service line)

- What is each competitor's distinct competitive market advantage?

- How are competitors positioned in the market?

- Who is the market leader? Why?

- What market share does each competitor hold? (in dollar value and unit volume)

- What market dynamics account for each competitor's current position in the market?

- How many competitors were in the market five years ago compared to today?

- What key marketing channels, if any, are utilized by each competitor?

- What new and anticipated market dynamics and competitor actions directly hinder, help, or otherwise have a direct impact on all competitors? How so? (examples: mergers, acquisitions, strategic partnerships, alliances, joint ventures, new products, sales strategies, cash infusion, strengths, weaknesses, and market opportunities)

- How does your pricing compare with your competitors'?

Format

Where possible, summarize competitor information in matrixes provided here. In the narrative highlight key findings and fill in any information gaps.

Table 2.8 Competitor Matrix by Organization

	Your Association	Competitor 1	Competitor 2	Competitor 3
Market entry	Year	Year	Year	Year
Organization type	Nonprofit	Dot.com	Distributor	Small business
Geography	Country	Region	State	Locale
No. of customers	#	#	#	#
Customer types	Individuals	Combination	Organizations	Combination
Targeted market segments	Descriptive name(s)	Descriptive name(s)	Descriptive name(s)	Descriptive name(s)
Organization culture	Board driven	Aggressive	Recently downsized	Start-up
Staff size	#	#	#	#
Annual sales	$	$	$	$
Market share	%	%	%	%
Market position	First in market Greatest longevity	Market challenger Most innovative	Lowest price	Largest product line Widest variety available
Strengths	Qualities/ characteristics	Qualities/ characteristics	Qualities/ characteristics	Qualities/ characteristics
Weaknesses	Qualities/ characteristics	Qualities/ characteristics	Qualities/ characteristics	Qualities/ characteristics
Opportunities	Circumstances/ conditions	Circumstances/ conditions	Circumstances/ conditions	Circumstances/ conditions
Threats	Circumstances/ conditions	Circumstances/ conditions	Circumstances/ conditions	Circumstances/ conditions
Market advantage				
Key marketing channels				
Other key competitive attributes				

Table 2.9   Competitive Product and Service Matrix

Company	Product/ Service	Market Entry	Feature/ Benefit 1	Feature/ Benefit 2	Feature/ Benefit 3	USP/ Competitive Advantage	Average Sales Price	Annual Sales Volume and/or Revenue
Your Association	Trade Name	Month/ Year	Comparative Descriptor	Comparative Descriptor	Comparative Descriptor	Key Message	$	$
Competitor 1								
Competitor 2								
Competitor 3								
Competitor 4								
Competitor 5								

Note: State the source of the information: month, year, and name of proprietary or published references.

Table 2.10   Competitor Pricing Analysis: Average Sales Price per Product or Service Unit

Product/Service	Average Sales Price				$ Increase/ Decrease Over Last	$ Increase/ Decrease Past 4 Years	% Increase/ Decrease Past 4 Years
	2005	2004	2003	2002			
Your Association Product/Service	$	$	$	$	+/−$	+/−$	+/−%
Competitor 1 Product/Service	$	$	$	$	+/−$	+/−$	+/−%
Competitor 2 Product/Service	$	$	$	$	+/−$	+/−$	+/−%
Competitor 3 Product/Service	$	$	$	$	+/−$	+/−$	+/−%

Note: State the source of the information: month, year, and name of proprietary or published references.

Chapter 3

Assess Your Association

*In oneself lies the whole world and if you know how to look
and learn, the door is there and the key is in your hand.*

—Krishnamurti

You've completed your examination of the significant factors of the external environment. The next step is to self-assess your organization's capabilities and resources.

Customer Profile

Who are the best customers and prospects for your association? The market segments you prioritize as the best fit for your association are your *target audiences*. How do you determine the best fit? In general, target audiences should be:

- **Identifiable.** The size and scope of the target audience can be defined and measured.

- **Accessible.** The target audience can be reached via your association's promotion and marketing channels.

- **Serviceable.** The size and nature of the target audience are such that your association possesses the resources to adequately service it.

- **Profitable.** The target audience is large enough and possesses enough buying power to be profitable for your association to pursue.

In addition, target audiences should be compatible with your association's strategic objectives and positioning. Of course it's easier to seek a market segment with the fewest competitors.

Formula

Start by examining member and customer data, market research findings and institutional knowledge (the firsthand experience you and your colleagues have with customers) to articulate your customer profile. Use the Customer or Target Market Profile Sheet (Table 3.1) as a guide for information to collect and fill in the chart.

Collect the same information about potential new market segments and compare those characteristics to the profile of your most profitable customers. This comparison helps you identify gaps to address in product development, promotion, and customer service. Test your selection of a potential market segment by asking whether the segment is identifiable, accessible, serviceable, and profitable, as well as compatible with your association's strategic objectives and positioning.

Format

An easy way to summarize your customer and prospect profile is shown in the Customer or Target Market Profile Sheet (Table 3.1).

SWOT Analysis

SWOT stands for *strengths, weaknesses, opportunities,* and *threats.* A SWOT analysis of your association provides a concise snapshot of current circumstances and specifically identifies what works and what doesn't work about your organization (or a competitor's) and its products and services.

Formula

Conducting the SWOT analysis is a clarifying exercise that will later support development of your marketing strategy. Strengths and weaknesses are *internal* organizational or product or service qualities to improve, leverage, or build upon; opportunities and threats are *external* market or environmental factors to exploit, protect against, or avoid.

In each category, first list the answers to each question in brief statements. Review your list and select recurrent patterns and significant obstacles to include in your SWOT analysis. Tell it like it is—no more, no less.

Strengths. Start on a positive note! What does your association do really well? What is absolutely terrific about your products and services? Consider these questions:

Table 3.1 Customer or Target Market Profile Sheet			
	Current Customers	**Target Market 1**	**Target Market 2**
Demographics			
Gender, age range			
Median income			
Highest degree achieved			
Marital status			
Professional title			
Years as member			
Leadership positions held			
Other characteristics			
Geographics			
Country			
State/region			
Locale			
Psychographics			
Attitudes			
Beliefs			
Opinions			
Personality			
Lifestyle			
Behaviorals			
Desired benefits/ motivations			
Product/service user status	Type of purchases		
Rate/frequency of product or service use	Frequency of purchases		
Degree of loyalty Repeat purchaser?	Number of annual purchases Value of annual purchases		
Readiness to buy			
Communication preferences	Mail, e-mail, telephone		

Note: State the source of the information: month, year, and name of proprietary or published references.

- How and why are we better than key competitors?

- What unique knowledge and experience does our staff possess?

- Where do we have a positive track record of success?

- What management practices are most effective?

- What resources (time, people, money, information, and technology) are available?

- Where do we demonstrate consistent efficiency?

- How are we innovative?

- What qualities do customers appreciate the most about our association?

- Why do customers prefer our products and services?

- How do we excel in customer service?

- Where do we consistently achieve or exceed our goals?

- How is our association a market leader?

Weaknesses. Problems and shortcomings exist in every association—in every business. The first step in overcoming weaknesses is identifying those negative conditions that block your ability to achieve goals. Consider the following questions and list all possibilities. What information is missing or incomplete?

- Which capabilities (management, fulfillment, and service) are substandard or absent?

- What resources (time, people, money, information, and technology) are depleted or lacking?

- How does the organizational structure and communication channels hinder performance?

- What policies or procedures are obsolete or faulty?

- What positive action(s) have we yet to pursue?

- Where do we consistently struggle or fail to meet our objectives?

- How do we frustrate our customers?

- What do our customers request that we can't or don't deliver?

- Where does performance quality suffer?

- What knowledge, experience, or training would make us more effectual?

- Are we poor in internal cooperation and collaboration and rich in petty politics?

- What sacred cows are we holding onto? Why?

Opportunities. Markets are by nature dynamic and new opportunities constantly evolve. In this section, identify market trends, conditions, or combinations of advantageous circumstances that will support achievement of your objectives. Consider the following questions:

- What new or alternative delivery channels could increase our profit margin?

- What challenges do our competitors face that we can leverage to our advantage?

- What unanticipated market circumstances work in our favor?

- Who in the marketplace could be a reliable ally or partner?

- What do customers want or need that we could provide?

- How can we take advantage of timing?

- Where do we have fresh entrée to market influencers and decision makers?

- What new markets or market niches do we have a clear chance to open?

- Who in the public's eye favors our cause?

- What media or public information outlets can we employ to increase awareness?

- What new technologies can we access cost effectively?

- How can we more effectively use the Internet?

Threats. No association is an island. We all operate in a larger market environment that's typically out of our direct control. In this section, identify trends and obstacles in your market environment that could prevent or delay achievement of your business objectives. Consider these questions:

- How could government regulations or pending legislation negatively affect us?

- How might competitors use our market positioning against us?

- Who or what in the marketplace intimidates us?

- Is the target audience shrinking or consolidating?

- Is overall supply increasing and demand decreasing?

- What alternative or new products or services are available to our customers (faster, cheaper, better)?

- What conditions make product or service delivery complicated, lengthy, or expensive?

- Will reliable marketing channels continue to be readily available?

- How would our customers acquire the same products or services if we ceased operation?

- What does the public misperceive or misunderstand about our organization?

- What myths do customers and prospects believe about our products or services?

- What warning signs indicate potentially hostile market conditions?

A SWOT analysis (see Table 3.2) is an effective way to understand your association's qualitative assets and liabilities and your market environment. An optional extension of the SWOT analysis involves conducting a Subjective Qualitative Analysis to compare the SWOT analysis of your association to that of competitors (Table 3.3). First identify the top ten characteristics to compare. Use your best judgment to assign a rating from one to ten for each organization on each characteristic. A rating of one indicates the organization is very weak, while ten indicates the organization is very strong in that area.

Total the scores for each organization and divide each score by the total number of characteristics to achieve an average score. While entirely subjective, this analysis provides a general relative indication of your association's overall performance compared to competitors.

Format

A SWOT analysis is best presented as a bulleted list of characteristics or in a chart like Table 3.2.

The subjective qualitative analysis can be presented in a chart like Table 3.3.

Table 3.2   Characteristics of a SWOT Analysis

	Positive	**Negative**
Internal	STRENGTHS 1. ... 2. ... 3. ... and so on	WEAKNESSES 1. ... 2. ... 3. ... and so on
External	OPPORTUNITIES 1. ... 2. ... 3. ... and so on	THREATS 1. ... 2. ... 3. ... and so on

Table 3.3   SWOT: The Subjective Qualitative Analysis

Characteristics to Compare	Your Association	Competitor 1	Competitor 2	Competitor 3
Characteristic 1				
Characteristic 2				
Characteristic 3				
Characteristic 4				
Characteristic 5				
Characteristic 6				
Characteristic 7				
Characteristic 8				
Characteristic 9				
Characteristic 10				
Totals				
Average Score (Total/10 = Avg. relative score)				

Product and Service Information

A *product* is a tangible item offered by your association with attributes that satisfy a customer need. Examples include magazines, research studies, buyers' guides, and the like. A *service* is an intangible product such as education seminars, membership, and certification programs. A *product or service line* is a group of products or services similar to each other in the way they are produced and marketed. For example, an association professional development department might offer a "line" of on-site education seminars and a "line" of distance-education programs.

Product or Service Description

Start with a concise summary definition of the product, service, or line of products or services. In a few paragraphs include the product or service trade name(s), category or type of product or service, availability, geographic market primary customers, and any other relevant or prominent descriptors.

Here is an example:

[Name of product or service] [trademark if applicable] is a *[descriptive characteristic (adjective)]*, *[descriptive characteristic (adjective)] [type of product/service (noun)]* for *[primary customers]* produced by *[name of organization]* and available in *[country, region, industry, or other market niche]* since *[date of inception or market entry]*.

Association Management™ is the premier four-color, monthly magazine for association professionals published by the American Society of Association Executives and available worldwide since 19XX.

Now expand the product or service description with information on the product or service life cycle stage, marketing channels, customer perceptions and sales, pricing, and revenue trends.

Product or Service Life Cycle

Successful products and services have a life cycle. Since marketing strategies are different for each stage of the *product life cycle*, your description should indicate the current life stage for each product or service. The four major stages of a product's life are:

Introductory stage. The first life stage of a product or service is generally characterized by minimal competition, limited market acceptance, and availability and promotion focused on informing target audiences. Pricing is set high to recover costs.

Growth stage. In the second stage, market acceptance, sales, and competition increase. Pricing remains high and profit margins are at a peak.

Maturity stage. By the third stage, the product or service is well known, with loyal customers and increasing direct competition.

Decline stage. In the final stage, sales are significantly decreased—often because market demand has dwindled, another product better satisfies customer needs, or a newer version of the product is available.

Marketing Channels

To cost effectively promote and deliver products and services to customers, your association may choose to enlist the support of other entities known as *marketing channels*. Marketing channels can provide value by extending your promotional reach and offering wider availability to customers.

For example, your association may utilize its components (often called chapters) as a marketing channel and offer monetary incentives based on sales, enrollment, or registration results. Or your association may distribute its line of textbooks via a for-profit company like Amazon.com in exchange for a percentage of the sales price.

The usefulness of a marketing channel will depend on your association's unique situation and how well the channel can complement or expand your accessibility and service to target audiences. If you choose to utilize marketing channels, be sure to identify them in all product or service descriptions.

Customer Perceptions

The only true value your product or service possesses exists in the mind of your customers. If your customers don't believe the product or service holds value, your marketing plan will need to address potential issues such as repackaging, repositioning, or sunsetting (retiring) the product or service. Bottom line, without customers there's no reason for a product or service to exist. It is therefore important to include information about how customers perceive and value the product or service. This can be accomplished concisely via a bulleted list addressing key issues as follows:

The current image and value many customers believe about the product or service include:

- Level of quality
- Functional performance

- Ease of acquisition and use

- Positive and negative associations

- Any misperceptions

- Overall satisfaction

Reminder: This isn't an opportunity to share your opinions, hopes, desires, and preferences regarding the product or service. Nor is it a chance to document what you imagine to be true about your customer. This isn't about you; it's about your customer. Rely on customer feedback, satisfaction surveys, and other market research to accurately define customer perceptions.

Sales, Pricing, and Revenue Trends

Next incorporate summary information on sales, pricing, and revenue trends in the past year as well as in comparison to the past three years. Answer these questions:

- How many units of the product or service were sold in the past twelve months? In each of the past three years? Examples: number of memberships, attendees, books, and subscriptions.

- How many dollars did we receive as a result in the past twelve months? In each of the past three years? Examples: amount of dues revenue, registration revenue, book sales, and subscription sales.

- What is the average sales price per unit during the past year? In each of the past three years? Examples: annual dues by member type, and individual registration fees by event type and customer type.

- What sales, pricing, and revenue trends did we experience in the past twelve months compared to the past three years?

- Are unit sales and pricing increasing or decreasing? How did that impact revenue?

Features, Advantages, and Benefits

Next, begin to outline the key attributes of each product or service.

Features	Advantages	Benefits
Attributes & Characteristics	Uniqueness	Favorable or Desired
Form		Customer Experience
Functionality		

Features are factual attributes or characteristics of a product or service expressed in terms of form or function. To define features, answer the questions:

- What is the product or service comprised of?

- How is the product or service structured, configured, or delivered?

- What does the product or service deliver?

- When or where is the product or service available?

Consider an association annual meeting. This service is typically *comprised of* a certain number of education sessions, networking events, and an exposition *structured* as an on-site event (versus an online or home-study video program) *delivering* education, experiences, information, and opportunities to buy *at* a specific location *on* specific dates.

Advantages distinguish what is unique or special about the features. For example, the location of the association annual meeting might offer customers ease of access by multiple travel methods. The education sessions might be unique due to targeted content, popularity of presenters, or wide variety. For each feature, answer the question: How is the product or service feature special or unique?

Benefits describe a favorable or desired experience the customer derives when using the product or service. Generally, customers purchase to avoid pain or gain pleasure. As consumers we are much more interested in the experience we'll get as a result of purchasing the product or service than the specific product or service features. This is especially true for association customers, since many offer intangible services (like membership and education) versus tangible products (widgets).

One customer might choose a distance education program over the annual meeting to avoid the pain of travel expenses and the inevitable catch-up after being away from the office. Conversely, another customer might choose the annual meeting to gain the pleasure of face-to-face peer networking experiences, group learning interactions, and the convenience and cost savings of previewing several vendors in one exposition.

To define benefits consider:

- What positive thought, emotion, or sensation does the customer experience?

- How will the customer avoid pain or gain pleasure?

■ How does the product or service improve users' ability to do what they want?

Format

Much of this information will be presented in narrative form, along with your FAB (Feature-Advantage-Benefit) Analysis for each product or service or line. Completing the worksheet allows you to thoroughly examine the product or service objectively, organize your thoughts, and eliminate assumptions. Later, this will also help you develop your marketing messages.

Table 3.4 Feature-Advantage-Benefit (F-A-B) Analysis			
Feature	**Advantages**	**Benefits**	**Marketing Messages**
List one factual attribute or characteristic of the product or service here.	Briefly describe what distinguishes the feature as unique or special.	What favorable or desired experience will the customer derive as a result of the feature and advantage?	What key phrases will be used to communicate the feature, advantage, and benefit to customers?
List another attribute here.	What makes this attribute special?	How will the customer avoid pain or gain pleasure?	What will we tell the customer?
List another attribute here . . . and so on.			

Chapter 4

Forecast Results

To accomplish great things, we must not only act,
but also dream; not only plan, but also believe.

—Anatole France, Novelist

N ow go get your crystal ball. It's time to foretell the future. At this stage of marketing planning, you and your colleagues must guess what will happen in the market and predict sales for the next twelve months. Seriously.

Did you think forecasting was a complicated mathematical science? Hardly! At best it's the science of guessing. Truthfully, you won't rely on SWAGs either. (*SWAG* is a technical statistics term for "silly wild a— guess," otherwise known as pulling numbers out of thin air.) Forecasting requires a balance of logic and intuition.

Think of the weather forecast. The local TV weather reporter with a bounty of meteorological apparatuses, data, language, and colorful, moving graphics leads us to actually believe how tomorrow will be. In fact, we routinely make decisions based on the information. They predict rain and we're sure to haul an umbrella to the office.

Is the weather forecast consistently and precisely accurate? Markets are no more controllable than the phenomenon of climate. By extension, while we have more command over sales results, ultimately it's only to the extent that we can effectively predict and respond to uncontrollable market dynamics. So, while forecasting is essentially formalized guesswork, thanks to your situation analysis and institutional knowledge gleaned from colleagues you'll be an "educated psychic" when predicting the market and your association's sales.

Key Issues

You've ferreted through a huge volume of information about your market and association. Now synthesize and summarize. Think strategically! Focus on issues that you anticipate will directly and significantly impact sales and should therefore be addressed when developing marketing strategies and tactics.

Formula

To introduce the forecast section of your marketing plan, summarize the top five market opportunities and challenges facing your association in the next twelve months.

The topics covered here depend entirely on the unique characteristics of your situation. Some questions to consider are:

- What economic, political, cultural, and technological factors will significantly impact association sales in the next twelve months? How? Why?

- What legislative or regulatory actions will influence our performance in the next twelve months? How? Why?

- What do market experts, analysts, and the media predict about the market in the next twelve months? How will that impact our association?

- In the next twelve months, what new or alternative products or services do we expect will influence customer behavior?

It's a good idea to solicit colleagues for their perspective regarding which issues are top priorities. Integrating their wisdom with factual data and your own experience ensures the marketing plan reflects and communicates a 360-degree view.

Format

First, articulate a brief summary statement outlining the key issue. Second, provide a bulleted list of the reasons why the key issues exists. Third, provide a bulleted list of the specific impact(s) on sales.

Here is an example:

Key issue summarized here.

Cause

- Identify the reason the situation is a key issue for your organization here.

- Identify another reason the situation is a key issue for your organization here.

- And so on.

Impact

- Identify the anticipated impact on your association's sales here.

- Identify another anticipated impact on your association's sales here.

- And so on.

Market Forecasts

A *market forecast* considers the prevailing market dynamics and predicts the total anticipated market universe (potential customers) and customer demand (sales). While primary market research can be useful, typically it's far too expensive for many corporations, much less nonprofit organizations. Finding an expert third-party opinion and other secondary market research combined with knowledge gleaned in your situation analysis is often your best bet.

Formula

Go back to the information you gathered in Chapter 2 (Understand the Market) about your market universe, share, growth, supply, and demand (Tables 2.3–2.7). Together these provide a snapshot of the past three to five years. Calculate percentage increases or decreases year to year and for all years reported. What are the trends?

- In the past three to five years has the market universe grown, declined, or remained static?

- In the past three to five years has the market growth rate remained flat, accelerated, or dropped?

- In the past three to five years has supply exceeded, met, or fallen short of demand?

Now consider the key issues summarized above. Given the history of the past three to five years and current market dynamics, answer the following questions:

- How do we expect the market universe to change in size and character in the next twelve months?

- At what rate do we anticipate the market will grow or decline in the next twelve months?

- What is the predicted product or service supply in the next twelve months?

- What is the predicted product or service demand in the next twelve months?

- How could your products or services change, be enhanced, or be extended to support increased sales?

Format. Much of this section can be presented in spreadsheet formats complemented by explanatory narrative as needed. The quantitative data in your market forecast will be incorporated into the annual sales forecast summaries described next.

Sales Forecasts

A *sales forecast* predicts total anticipated sales and related revenue to your organization by market segment for a specific period of time (typically one year). Typical methodologies for sales forecasts include:

Customer focused approach (recommended). This approach considers your association's actual sales and market share history combined with prevailing market dynamics. Also called *bottom-up* or *build-up* method.

Ivory tower approach (least effective yet most common in associations). This approach uses your association's objectives rather than market information as a basis.

Rolling forecast (recommended for new product launches). Sales are predicted for the first three months (month 1, month 2, and month 3) and the subsequent three calendar quarters (quarter 2, quarter 3, and quarter 4). At the end of month 3, actual sales results are considered to repredict quarter 2, in terms of months (month 4, month 5, month 6), and an initial prediction for quarter 5 is made. The advantage is that you can adjust sales forecasts frequently and also retain a twelve-month forecast. The disadvantage is that you also need to adjust your budget on a quarterly basis.

Market test (expensive). Ask your customers when and how much they plan to buy. While primary market research such as this can be useful it's very expensive. Also, consumer product experts say the 20 percent rule applies; that is, for every 100 people who say they will buy only 20 actually do.

Institutional knowledge and experience (recommended in concert with customer focused approach). You and your colleagues are likely (or should be) close to your customers and familiar with market dynamics. Soliciting opinions of your colleagues, particularly those with tenure in your organization, will provide unique insight into your association and its culture, trends, and capabilities.

Find out what metrics your association currently uses to estimate sales and revenue, and how each department or functional area contributes to the organization's total financial projection. Share the information you've gleaned from the situation analysis and collaborate to develop forecasts. Engaging your colleagues in this process helps alleviate the common scenario of competing goals or varying market assumptions among internal departments.

For example, with tangible products Marketing generally prefers greater supply than actual demand to ensure customers are happy. (For example, Administration fulfills customer orders as promptly as possible.) A pessimistic forecast means revenue shortfalls due to a lack of product availability. Lost customers are far more difficult for Marketing to recover. An overly optimistic forecast means cash is tied up in inventory. Finance is pressured to keep COGs (cost of goods) low and directs Administration to minimize inventories. Marketing doesn't feel the pain when Finance and Administration is squeezed and Finance and Administration doesn't understand why Marketing can't forecast accurately.

By collaborating with colleagues you help ensure sales and revenue forecasts are as credible as possible and supported by everyone in the association. Without this agreement from your colleagues, the marketing plan stands little chance of acceptance or adoption by the organization.

Formula

If a formula doesn't exist in your association, here's a simple approach to calculate sales forecasts:

Step 1. Identify actual sales history for each product or service from the past three years and compile findings into the Annual Sales Forecast Summary for a Product or Service Type (Table 4.1). Consider the historical sales trends for each product or service, and project annual sales over the next three years. Initially the projection is your best guess based on key assumptions learned through your situation analysis combined with the actual sales history.

Step 2. Compile annual forecasts for all products and services into the Sales Forecast Summary by Market Segment and Product or Service (Table 4.2). Individual product or service volume (units), revenue (dollars), and average

Year	Total Market Volume (units)	Association Market Share (%)	Association Product Sales (volume)	Association Product Average Sales Price	Association Product Sales (revenue)
Table 4.1		**Annual Sales Forecast Summary for a Product or Service Type (Sales Forecast Step 1)**			
Actual Sales					
2000	1675	15%	251	$200	$50,250
2001	1750	17%	298	$225	$66,938
2002	1800	14.7%	265	$225	$59,535
Sales Forecasts					
2003	2000	15.0%	300	$225	$67,500
2004	2100	15.0%	315	$225	$70,875
2005	2205	15.0%	331	$225	$74,419

Assumptions:

1. Total market for Product/Service 1 will continue to expand at a growth rate of 5% per year.
2. Association will maintain an average market share of 15.5% per year for Product/Service 1.
3. Average sales price for Product/Service 1 will remain constant through 2005.

sales price forecasts go in the columns "total forecast all segments" and "average sales price."

Step 3. Divide the total volume and revenue forecasts for each product or service into specific market segments, based on what portion of the total forecast you expect each market segment to purchase. Calculate totals by market segment.

Double check. As a double-check, compare your sales forecasts by market segment with actual sales derived from each market segment in the past three to five years. Adjust as appropriate. There may be unique market dynamics that cause you to stick with your projected forecast. Be sure to explain your assumptions in the narrative.

Table 4.2   Sales Forecast Summary by Market Segment and Product or Service (Sales Forecast Steps 2 and 3)

	Market Segment 1	Market Segment 2	Market Segment 3	Total Forecast All Segments	Average Sales Price
Product/Service 1: XYZ Seminar					
Unit Forecast: No. of Registrations	150	100	50	300	
$ Forecast: No. of Registrations × Average Sales Price	$33,750	$22,500	$11,250	$67,500	$225
Product/Service 2					
Unit forecast	250	300	250	800	
Sales forecast	$37,500	$45,000	$37,500	$120,000	$150
Product/Service 3					
Unit forecast	75	100	125	300	
Sales forecast	$6,000	$8,000	$10,000	$24,000	$80
Total unit forecast	475	500	425	1,400	
Total sales forecast	$77,250	$75,500	$58,750	$211,500	

Step 4. Depending on how your association tracks sales, you may need to break down the sales forecast summary by market segment and product or service into monthly or quarterly projections (again, see Table 4.2). Because of the volume of information, this is best presented in a spreadsheet.

Step 5. Collaborate with colleagues to compare your initial forecasts and supporting data with their best guesses. Adjust the projection based on their input and any additional information that becomes available. It's best to arrive at realistic numbers the entire organization can agree to support.

Format

It's important to use a consistent formula to develop forecasts year to year so that the numbers are relevant to each other. Much of this section can be presented in spreadsheets with explanatory narrative as needed.

Chapter 5

Set Objectives

Failure comes only when we forget our ideals and objectives and principles.

—Jawaharlal Nehru

If you don't know where you are going, you might wind up someplace else.

—Yogi Berra

How do you spell *success*? With specific measurable goals! Objectives in your marketing plan define what you intend to achieve by when. Your objectives are based on your situation analysis and serve as the bull's-eye your marketing plan is aimed to hit.

Objectives must be:

- Specific: Define a precise result to be achieved.

- Measurable: Define the extent, degree, quality, or amount of achievement numerically.

- In time: Define the exact date by which the result will be achieved.

- Aligned: Support achievement of the association's strategic goals

Generally, objectives fall into two categories: business objectives and marketing objectives.

Business Objectives

Business objectives are goals that indicate financial performance, such as gross sales volume or revenue, net sales volume or revenue, average sales price, market share, gross profit, gross margin, and contribution margin.

You can use these measures for specific product or service lines, and your association will likely use some of these measures to calculate the organization's overall performance and profitability. It's a good idea to find out what indicators the association currently uses to measure success. Depending on your association's specific circumstances, certain measures may be more or less important. Often you may need to align with existing measures as well as introduce the use of new metrics that more accurately measure specific marketing initiatives.

Formula

Here's how to understand and calculate performance indicators for business objectives. First let's review key terms so you better understand the calculations that follow.

Gross sales volume is the total number of units sold. In associations this could include number of annual memberships, event registrations, or publication subscriptions.

Gross sales revenue equals total dollars generated from total number of units sold.

Average sales price is the average per unit dollar cost to the customer.

Market share represents the percentage of the total market universe your organization owns. This ratio may be expressed in terms of number of customers or sales volume or revenue.

Net sales is calculated as

> Gross Sales Volume or Revenue − Returns + Bad or Damaged Product = Net Sales Volume or Revenue. This measures the total value in terms of volume or revenue of all "good" sales transactions.

Gross profit, also known as *net revenue on sales,* is calculated as

> Net Sales Revenue − Cost of Sales = Gross Profit Dollars.

Cost of sales is also known as cost of goods sold (COGS) and includes merchandise purchase costs, freight, and production costs.

Gross margin, also known as *gross profit margin,* is calculated as

> Gross Profit ÷ Net Sales Revenue = Percentage of Gross Margin.

The ratio measures your ability to simultaneously control costs, sustain or increase sales, and sustain or increase sales prices. A decline in the gross margin of a product might indicate a problem in inventory management or that pricing lags behind cost of goods sold.

Contribution margin, also known as *net profit margin* or *net margin,* is

> Net Sales Revenue − Total Variable Costs (COGS, sales commissions, marketing expenses) ÷ Net Sales Revenue = Contribution Margin.

This ratio shows the percentage of each sales dollar that is true profit to your association.

Develop your business objectives, then test against these questions:

- Is the result to be achieved expressed clearly enough that my mom will understand it?

- What information, reports, or calculation will I use to determine whether the result was completely (or partially) achieved?

- By when will the result be achieved?

- What would failure look like?

Format

A bulleted list of brief statements is best. Rule of thumb: Your entire list of business objectives should fit on a T-shirt and require no more time than an elevator ride to recite. Here are a few examples:

- Increase publication gross sales revenue by 10 percent over last year by December 31, 2002.

- Maintain average sales price at $135 per education seminar through June 30, 2002.

- Enroll 5,000 new members by December 31, 2002.

Marketing Objectives

While they are as specific and measurable as business objectives, marketing objectives also address other qualitative and management issues such as product development, licensing, staffing, market research, and budget management. For example, if you increase gross sales revenue but spend five times more than the allocated budget, it can hardly be called a win.

New product and service launches require substantial preparatory work and tap the expense budget without contributing to revenue. Recruiting and retaining marketing staff is an essential management activity, especially if your association is short-handed or was recently reorganized.

Formula

Your marketing objectives should reflect goals that are specific, measurable, and support profitability and effective association marketing management but that may not be evident in financial performance indicators. Examples could include marketing initiatives such as:

- Proffering and negotiating strategic partnerships and alliances

- New product and service development

- New product and service launches

- Recruiting and retaining key staff

- Managing a database conversion

- Association merger, consolidation, or reorganization

Develop your marketing objectives, then test against these questions:

- Is the result to be achieved expressed clearly enough that my mom will understand it?

- What information, reports, or calculation will I use to determine whether the result was completely (or partially) achieved?

- By when will the result be achieved?

- What would failure look like?

Format

A bulleted list of brief statements is best. Rule of thumb: As with your business objectives, your entire list of marketing objectives should fit on a T-shirt and require no more time than an elevator ride to recite. Here are a few examples of marketing objectives:

- Hire and train two new marketing representatives by March 30, 2002, to support customer retention and acquisition in the United States and Canada.

- Develop and launch one new education product by July 1, 2002.

- Negotiate and sign strategic partnerships with five business corporations by December 31, 2003.

Chapter 6

Create Positioning

*Don't overlook the importance of worldwide thinking.
A company that keeps its eye on Tom, Dick, and Harry
is going to miss Pierre, Hans, and Yoshio.*

—Al Reis, Marketer

Good positioning is like General Mills achieving success in the cereal aisle at the grocery store. Like most companies that vie for consumer sales, General Mills, Post, and Kellogg's compete vigorously for the maximum amount of shelf space. Why? Because consumers are more likely to buy from their companies if more of their products can be easily viewed and reached.

The same is true of positioning your organization. The average person sees 6,000 marketing messages daily, according to the Advertising Research Foundation—even more if you walk down a cereal aisle! Remember, the only true value your product or service possesses exists in the mind of your customers. Positioning is what determines where your product, service, or organization message is placed on the mental shelf in your customer's mind and how distinct it is from competitors' messages.

Here's how other experts define positioning:

"The way the product is defined by consumers on important attributes—the place the product occupies in consumers' minds relative to competing products."

—Philip Kotler, 1999

"Designing a marketing program that customers will perceive as desirable and that will give a firm an advantage over current and potential competitors."

—Harper W. Boyd & Orville C. Walker, 1990

Positioning articulates the most sustainable benefit(s) that give the greatest leverage for the product or service and that cannot be owned by any competitor. Here are a few easy examples:

Volvo positions its automobiles around safety, Toyota positions them around economy and value for the dollar, and BMW positions them around high performance.

Formula

Developing a positioning statement for each product or service line is an important element of your marketing plan. After all, if your association doesn't clearly define and own a position in the marketplace, your competitors will do it for you! Plus, how will you ever communicate value to your prospects and customers if you're not aware of it? Remember, from the customer's perspective, products and services are a group of tangible and intangible characteristics including packaging, price, brand, and service.

Customers will place your products, services, and organization in their minds whether you influence their perspective or not. In order to control how your customers and prospects perceive your association and its products and services, a consistent marketing position should be evident throughout the entire marketing mix and directly support marketing strategies.

Every product or service can be positioned in multiple ways using a variety of strategies such as:

- Product or service features or advantages

- Benefits for target audiences

- Usage or accessibility

- Customer group or type

- Against a competitor

- First to market

- Only or one-of-a-kind

The best positioning statement, also known as a *unique selling proposition,* or *USP,* emphasizes the feature, advantage, or benefit that cannot be claimed by competitors and that directly fulfills your target audience's wants and needs. For example, the positioning statement for the ASAE ASSOCIATION MANAGEMENT™ magazine is "to be the trusted provider of compelling, relevant, and timely editorial content to the association community."

To construct a positioning statement, consider these questions:

- What is standing in the way of moving prospects or customers from what they currently think to what we *want* them to think?

- What is the single, most sustainable benefit that cannot be owned by any competitor?

- What single, net impression or attitude, if adopted by the target audiences, will move them to make the desired behavior change?

- What do we want the target audience to think and do as a result of our communication?

Format

Articulated as a clear, concise statement or paragraph, your positioning statement should incorporate what is unique about your products or services compared to competitors', and it should emphasize those attributes of greatest value to target audiences that no other product or service is perceived to possess. A good positioning statement includes:

- Target audiences

- Kind of product or service

- Most compelling product or service benefit(s)

- How your product or service is different (and better) than competitors'

Sample format 1. [*Name of product or service*] [*trademark if applicable*] is the [*type of product or service (noun)*] of choice because it provides [*benefit*], [*benefit*], and [*benefit*] that [*target audience(s)*] demand at a lower cost.

Sample format 2. [*Name of product or service*] [*trademark if applicable*] offers the most [*advantage or benefit (adjective)*] [*type of product or service (noun)*] available for [*primary customers*]. [*Name of product or service*] is only produced by [*name of organization*] and available in [*country, region, industry, or other market niche*] since 19XX.

Chapter 7

Develop Strategies and Tactics

*I am the world's worst salesman; therefore, I
must make it easy for people to buy.*

—Sam Walton, Wal-Mart

Strategies

Marketing strategies are the logic you use to position the association in the market and achieve the business and marketing objectives, given the situation analysis.

Formula

First recall (or better yet, re-read) the discussion in Chapter 1 on the four Ps versus the four Cs and consider how this applies to your association. Here is a five-step, relational thinking exercise to get your wheels turning, because it focuses your attention on those aspects of your business that most need to be addressed with marketing strategies. You'll need to refer to the SWOT analysis charts you prepared for your association and key competitors. Consider the questions indicated under each step.

Step 1. Identify broad strategic goals.

- What are the association's broad strategic goals as outlined in the strategic plan?

- What general approach does the association intend to take this year to meet its strategic goals?

Typically, strategic goals fall into one of four categories:

1. *Market penetration*, an approach focused on gaining and retaining a greater share of existing targeted markets (such as, we aim to get and keep relationships with more customers).

2. *Product development*, an approach focused on developing more products or services to sell to existing target audiences (such as, we want to fulfill a broader range of our customers' wants or needs in new ways).

3. *Market development*, an approach focused on selling existing products or services to brand-new target markets. (For example, let's figure out who else wants or needs our products or services and form a relationship with them.)

4. *Diversification*, an approach with simultaneous focus on new target markets and more products. Existing, modified, and new products are sold in existing and new markets at the same time. (For example, let's form and keep relationships with our primary target audience, find new and different targets to build relationships with, sell our existing products or services to both, and invent new products or services for both.)

Step 2. Use strengths to neutralize threats.

■ What strengths does the association possess that neutralize threats from competitors and market dynamics?

Step 3. Build on strengths to leverage opportunities.

■ What strengths does the association possess that can help us take advantage of our opportunities?

Step 4. Overcome weaknesses that aggravate threats.

■ How can the association improve those weak spots that would help a threat from our competitors or the market to actualize?

Step 5. Choose offense or defense.

■ Will a good "offense" or good "defense" help us use our strengths to neutralize threats, build on strengths to leverage opportunities, and overcome weaknesses that aggravate threats?

As in sports, in marketing there are offensive and defensive strategies. Developing offensive marketing strategies requires you to anticipate and take action accordingly. For example, you foresee customer wants and needs (via market research) and then develop an offensive customer strategy to adjust association products or services to meet those needs before or better than competitors. Or you know (via market research) how potential customers think, feel, and experience the association and then design an offensive communication strategy to build awareness of the mission, clarify any misperceptions, and engender loyalty.

Defensive marketing strategies are reactive in nature—typically in response to competitor activities or market dynamics. For example, you design a defensive cost strategy of incentives (lower sales prices; discounts; buy one, get one free) to attract customers away from competitors. Or, you utilize new or expanded marketing channels to increase the customer's opportunity to buy from your association versus competitors as a defensive convenience strategy.

Format

Strategies are expressed in narrative form, followed by all tactics related to the strategy in priority order. Be sure the priority of your strategies tracks with the expense priorities in your marketing budget. As you develop appropriate marketing strategies for your unique situation, consider the following common strategic approaches:

- Target a specific market segment where your competitor is weak.

- Challenge the market leader in multiple ways simultaneously to erode competition and thereby capture market share.

- Follow the market leader to minimize risk while maintaining market share.

- Stimulate customers to stay loyal, try products and services, and purchase more via incentives.

- Bypass competition by diversifying products and services.

- Adapt domestic activities for international markets.

- Identify and strengthen your weaknesses with targeted market segments.

- Anticipate competitor attacks and position yourself to prevent, delay, or minimize any negative impact.

- Build awareness and loyalty by promotion of image and mission.

- Expand or diversify marketing channels.

- Partner with competitors to cross-market noncompeting products and services.

Tactics

Tactics are the specific marketing approaches, methods, and actions employed to implement a strategy. Generally, tactics can be described as *push, pull,* or *push-pull* in relation to your target audiences. Push tactics are characteristically "top-down" and "inside-out," in that focus originates with the organization and moves out to target audiences. Pull tactics are characteristically "bottom-up" and "outside-in," in that the organization's focus originates with the target audience (as opposed to itself).

For example, to implement a diversification strategy, a customer push approach prioritizes your association's capabilities and preferences as the fundamental basis for new product or service development. A pull approach for product development would first focus on target audience wants and needs and adjust the association to meet the market demand. A push-pull approach would consider your association's capabilities and market demand equally important.

A push communication tactic promotes to marketing channels that in turn sell or push your products or services directly to end users. In contrast, pull communications promote directly to end users to attract or pull customers toward your association (versus a competitor) to purchase. Push-pull communications promote to end users and marketing channels simultaneously.

The tactics you'll use depend on the strategy they support. For example, to support a market penetration strategy you want tactics designed to get existing customers to spend more money more frequently. For promotion purposes it makes more sense to select direct mail over advertising because you already own the customer information necessary to communicate directly with decision makers. You can go right in your prospects' front door, rather than waiting for them to respond to an advertisement.

Here's an overview of key marketing tactics:

Customer (or product). Your association's mix of products or services is interdependent with customer wants or needs and is influenced by cost (price), convenience (place), and communication (promotion) tactics. Common approaches to consider include:

Modification: Adjusting the features of an existing product or service to better satisfy changing, expanded, or new customer wants or needs.

Extension: Offering customers more choice by introducing new features and advantages to an existing or modified product or service.

Development: Identifying new, additional, or different customer wants or needs and inventing new products or services to fulfill those wants or needs. This approach is often essential when existing products or services are in the declining stage of their life cycle.

Sunsetting: Deciding to drop products or services that no longer adequately satisfy customer wants or needs and are therefore no longer profitable.

Cost (or price). The pricing of your association's products or services is interdependent with the customers' perception of value and is influenced by customer (product), convenience (place), and communication (promotion) tactics. *Price* is the amount of money you ask the customer to pay for products or services.

Generally, pricing is described as "elastic" or "inelastic" in relation to the customer's perceived value of the product or service. Elasticity speaks to the customers' degree of sensitivity to price and their resulting demand for a product or service. Price-elastic customers are sensitive or responsive to changes in price. Price-inelastic customers are not sensitive or responsive to changes in price. High elasticity means there is increased market demand when price changes; low elasticity means there is no change in market demand when price changes. Common approaches to consider include:

Premium value. Customers perceive the product or service as superior quality, exclusive, prestigious, or otherwise of high value and, as a result, are willing to pay high premium prices. This approach is appropriate for price-inelastic market segments.

Volume penetration. A large pool of potential purchasers (who want or need and can afford the product or service) exists and may select multiple competitors from which to buy. As a result, your organization sets a low price to capture market share. This approach is appropriate for price-elastic market segments.

Complementary. Customers are offered multiple products or services in a single purchase. Pricing of one product or service is optimal for the customer to increase usage and demand for another product or service.

Comparative or competitive. Pricing is based on similar products or services offered by competitors, as opposed to consideration of demand or production costs. For example, an organization attempts to undercut competitors by slashing prices for a particular geographic market or for a limited period of time—or an organization adopts the market leader's prices.

Cost plus. The simplest approach, whereby the fixed and variable costs associated with a product or service are added together with a standard markup, regardless of market demand or competition.

Convenience (or place). Your association's mix of marketing channels is interdependent with customer preferences for acquiring products or services and is influenced by customer or product, cost or price, and communication or promotion tactics. Common approaches to consider include:

Extensive. A large pool of potential purchasers with high demand for convenience exists in diverse geographic locations, and an organization owns the capacity to mass-produce and distribute products or services through as many marketing channels as possible.

Selective. A pool of potential purchasers with moderate demand for convenience exists in targeted geographic locations, and an organization produces enough to satisfy most customer needs, distributing products or services via a limited number of marketing channels.

Exclusive. An organization limits distribution to one outlet, with or without regard to market demand.

Communication (or promotion). Your association's mix of marketing communications is interdependent with customer preferences for gathering information about products or services and interacting with your association. Customer or product, cost or price, and convenience or place tactics also influence marketing communications. Common approaches to consider include:

Advertising. Printed or broadcast public notices and announcements that tell about a product, service, organization, cause, or other matter. Examples include magazine and newspaper display advertising, online banner ads, radio and TV commercials, billboard and public transit signs, postcard decks, broadcast fax, and classified or yellow pages listings.

Celebrity endorsement. A well-known person agrees to publicly endorse an organization, cause, product, or service. This approach typically is used in conjunction with other communication tactics. A good example is NBC *Today*

Show coanchor Katie Couric's endorsement of the National Colorectal Cancer Research Alliance of the Entertainment Industry Foundation.

Customer service. How you keep customers happy! Includes your philosophy, procedures, and methods for interacting with customers.

Direct mail. Promotional information sent to target audiences in the mail. Examples include letters, newsletters, coupons, catalogs, and statement stuffers. This approach requires ownership or rental of target audience lists containing names, addresses, and other descriptors. Testing appeals on a small number of prospects is recommended to ensure the most effective selling message. Average response rate is 1 percent to 3 percent of the total number of mailers sent.

Direct selling. Involves one-on-one sales presentations to potential customers. Examples include face-to-face and door-to-door sales as well as outbound and inbound telemarketing.

Incentives. Special offers designed to motivate customers to buy more, sooner, or repeatedly. Typically, they are used to support other communication tactics. Examples include free and trial samples, free gifts, contests, coupons, and discounts.

Internet. Examples include outbound e-mail, Web sites, and e-commerce.

Partnerships. Aligning with other organizations to accomplish mutual goals. Examples include cooperative communications campaigns (such as co-op advertising and public relations), joint ventures, and alliances.

Point-of-purchase collateral. Print or electronic materials designed to educate and persuade prospects to buy. Typically, they are used in conjunction with other communication tactics. Examples include sales brochures, data sheets, rate cards, signage, posters, and audiovisuals.

Premiums. Specialty items featuring a logo and designed to maintain awareness of a product, service, or organization. Typically, they are used to support other communication tactics. Examples include novelties such as baseball caps, coffee mugs, T-shirts, pens and pencils, toys, and other giveaways.

Public relations. Involves public communications designed to shape and increase positive awareness of the association's image and products or services. Examples include business cards and letterhead, Web site, press releases, feature stories, letters to the editor, public service announcements, talk radio and TV shows, annual reports, press conferences, and lobbying activities. Value to an organization increases over time with sustained effort.

Special events. Examples include trade shows, educational seminars, product presentations, and entertainment.

Word of mouth. What your customers say to other potential customers. This is entirely dependent upon all aspects of the marketing mix and relies on consistently matching and meeting customer expectations.

Formula

To determine the most appropriate tactics to support each strategy, consider the following questions for each type of tactic:

Customer or Product

- How effectively does the product or service meet target audiences' wants or needs?

- What adjustments or revisions to the product or service would better meet target audiences' wants or needs?

- At what life cycle stage is the product or service?

- Are close substitutes or alternatives readily available to target audiences?

- Is meeting customer demand more cost-effective if the product or service is pushed via marketing channels or pulled via advertising?

- What are the plans for new product development?

Cost or Pricing

- Are target audiences price-elastic or price-inelastic?

- What is the market demand?

- What is our pricing objective?

- What factors regarding the target audience influence this pricing decision?

- Is the price method focused on long-term or short-term gains?

- How will the price set for a product or service influence customer perception and satisfaction?

- How do our prices compare with competitors' pricing on similar products or services?

Convenience or Place

■ How do target audiences prefer to acquire the product or service?

■ What marketing channels are best suited to meet customer demands for availability and convenience?

■ How do selected marketing channels influence customer cost?

■ Can we effectively deliver an increased volume of products or services while maintaining quality customer service?

Communications or Promotion

■ How do target audiences prefer to receive information about our products or services?

■ What mix of communications allows the most frequent and cost-effective interaction with target audiences?

■ How many individuals in our target audience are online?

■ Who in the public's eye supports our mission or benefits from our work? Will they lend endorsement?

■ To support the strategy, do we need communications to generate fast response, build awareness, or a combination of both?

Format

Tactics are presented in narrative form under each strategy the tactic supports. Tactics should be clearly defined in terms of the method, timing, and target audiences. For day-to-day management purposes, it's a good practice to develop a separate document that re-prioritizes tactics by date and indicates the person responsible for the tactic. See Appendix 3 for a sample action plan format.

Chapter 8

Identify Resource Requirements

Seek not, my soul, the life of the immortals;
but enjoy to the full the resources that are within thy reach.

—Pindar

The major resources you'll need to implement your marketing plan include time, people, money, information, and technology.

Time

As you've learned, it takes a lot of time, energy, and focus to develop and implement your marketing plans. Despite best intentions, a rare organization that accomplishes everything set forth in an annual marketing plan. Of course, there's a better chance you'll get more done with a marketing plan than without one. If the plan is implemented effectively, you're absolutely more likely to achieve revenue goals. And it's important to be realistic. Just as there are boundaries on your staff count and budget there are a finite number of hours in a day. Work too much and you'll lose your sense of well-being. Get lazy and you'll lose your job.

Formula

Be practical about the time allotted to implement elements of your plan—particularly expenses. You can probably find a printer to produce a brochure in 48 hours, but it will cost you a fortune in rush charges. See Table 8.1 for several rules of thumb to develop a realistic project timeline.

Also, plan for breakdowns. As you develop your tactical action plan, anticipate that all will not go exactly as you envisioned. Unforeseen priorities pop

Table 8.1   Marketing Implementation Time by Tactic

Tactic	Variables	Number of Weeks
Planning		
Marketing plan development	Quality, age, and relevance of market research Staff availability	4 to 12 weeks
Market Research		
Market research study	Size, scope, methodology	8 to 40 weeks
Customer satisfaction mail questionnaire	Size, scope	4 to 8 weeks
E-survey		1 to 2 weeks
Creative		
Copywriting: Direct mail packages, brochures, magazine articles	Clarity of concept development, complexity of offer, knowledge of target audience	2 to 3 weeks
Graphic design: Direct mail packages, brochures, newsletters	Clarity of concept development, complexity, volume of text and images, author's alterations	3 weeks
Graphic design: product catalogs, directories	Clarity of concept development, complexity, volume of text and images, author's alterations	4 to 6 weeks
Logo design Cover design (book, magazine)	Clarity of brand concept, author's alterations, number of approvals	6 to 12 weeks
Web site design	Clarity of concept, development, integration with existing systems	6 to 12 weeks
Production		
List acquisition	Size of list rental, output format, approval of mail package, payment method and timing	2 to 4 weeks
Data processing	Size/accuracy of mail list Requirements for merge/purge, zip code correction, suppression, address standardization, random selection, output format	5 to 10 days

Table 8.1 (*continued* on the following page)

Table 8.1 (*continued* from the previous page)		
Tactic	**Variables**	**Number of Weeks**
Printing	Calibration between designer's file set-up and printer's prepress operations, author's alterations	3 to 4 weeks
Mail shop	Number and type of mail pieces, addressing method, number of components in mail package, requirements for matching, postal processing/USPS class, drop shipping Method of postage payment Service provider's volume capabilities and current production availability	5 to 10 days
Promotions		
Direct mail response time		2 to 6 weeks
Annual meeting marketing and promotion		15 to 18 months prior to event date

up, breakdowns do happen, people get sick, and technology suffers glitches. You will also encounter the inevitable "project from hell" that gobbles up time and other resources without much in the way of results. Add an extra week to complete every project and your plan will be more realistic.

In associations where marketing is a centralized function, it's particularly important to negotiate and publish an agreed-upon timetable with each program manager well in advance. This helps ensure a product or service is actually developed by the time you need to start promoting it.

One classic example is event marketing. It's tough to develop a unique selling position (benefits) for an education seminar when the organization is still scrambling to find speakers and coordinate content. Consider developing a simple flowchart that incorporates the product development as well as promotion to keep everyone informed of the general timing for marketing initiatives.

It also takes time and constancy to nurture and sustain profitable relationships with prospects and customers. Give your marketing strategies time to work. Just because the organization wants 10,000 new members doesn't mean a member-add-a-member campaign can generate those results in twelve months. Big goals require sustained, committed action over time. Most strategies need more than twelve months to mature and be fully productive. Think beyond the next twelve months and ensure the current marketing plan also builds a foundation for future marketing success.

Format

The Daily Marketing Action Plan (Appendix 3) will help you prioritize tactics in time. A less detailed version of this chart can also be provided to colleagues to keep everyone apprised of marketing initiatives. Consider a marketing plan for each product or service as a handy reference when implementing tactics.

People

Ever feel like your plate is too small for the buffet your association serves up? Ever wish for even one pair of extra hands to manage your workload? Notoriously understaffed, associations constantly grapple with staffing. After all, it costs the association much more than salary to hire employees. The benefits package and overhead expenses typically cost an additional 15 to 30 percent per person, not to mention the human investment required in managing multiple personalities for peak performance. All that adds up.

Formula

Your association may not be willing or able to commit additional staff for marketing initiatives. If that's the reality ask yourself: Is it truly possible to accomplish your marketing plan with the current staff resources? If not, how could you adjust your marketing plan to do more with less?

Outsourcing is one viable solution that most associations (and corporations) are adopting. Essentially, outsourcing frees up an organization to focus on its core competencies—what they do best. You hire independent firms or contractors whose expertise fills the association's non-core functions specifically. You gain the benefit of targeted expertise at the right time without the extra burden of salary and benefits. As the client, you gain greater flexibility and freedom. It's much easier to extricate yourself from a relationship with a service provider compared to an employee. You still call the shots. Service providers are motivated to give you what you want because their fee is tied to a specific deliverable. Outsourcing is a common, affordable association practice for any size organization.

Format

Include a narrative explanation of the resources required and options available.

Information

As associations face more competition from the corporate world, more of them are turning to proven business marketing principles and practices to sustain and grow the organization. Information derived from primary market research is a core resource to stay competitive.

Formula

Although many nonprofit organizations are finally catching on, many still don't have a clue about research. Allocate time, people, and money for market research in every marketing plan you craft—not just for customer satisfaction surveys or annual meeting feedback forms.

Even if your association can only afford one study annually, begin to build information resources to make smarter decisions in the future. Where should you start? Look to your situation analysis. What data was missing or really difficult to find? Start by filling the gaps. Then consider what additional data you'll need for future planning.

Marketing is a discipline pervading every function of an organization. For effective marketing planning you'll need to know and understand how every aspect of the association's business interrelates. You're also responsible for communicating marketing information to all areas of the business. Don't assume that your colleagues understand the market as well as you, or that you know more than they do. Educate. Share information.

One of the most common problems in implementing marketing plans is lack of awareness, which fosters misunderstanding, which leads to lack of cooperation. Communication is a two-way interaction: Sender and receiver are 100 percent responsible for delivering and receiving the message. Seek and utilize input, feedback, and institutional knowledge. And keep colleagues informed throughout implementation!

Format

An explanation of the resources required can be presented in narrative form.

Technology

Be sure to consider technology needs when developing your marketing plan. Did your situation analysis reveal the need for more customer data? Do you need a new database to effectively segment and track customer information? Can the reports you need be accomplished with simple programming changes by your IT department? Are there effective controls in place to measure marketing results? What policies and procedures need to be revised? These are larger questions that often require significant resources.

Formula

Surely you won't get the resources if the organization doesn't know you need them. While it's sometimes tempting to avoid controls and measurements, identifying technology needs for effective marketing decision making is essential.

Format

An explanation of the resources required can be presented in narrative form.

Money

Time, people, information, and technology all need to be considered as you develop your marketing budget—another key tactic of your marketing plan. Most associations have an annual budget development process and specific budget formats appropriate to their financial accounting system, so there's no need to reinvent the wheel. However, it's a good idea to be familiar with the more common budgeting methods including the following.

Percentage of sales. This method determines the marketing budget for a specific period of time, based on a percentage of actual sales derived during a previous period of time.

Fixed sum per unit. This method allocates a set dollar amount for each product or service unit produced for a given time period. The dollar amount multiplied by the number of units equals the marketing expense limits for that time period.

Objective and task. This budgeting approach calculates the cost of marketing activities against the results forecast.

Ivory tower method. This approach relies solely on the judgment of a few with little input from many. Asking potential employers about their preferred budgeting method is always an interesting interview question.

Formula

As you construct your budget it's important to:

- Start by building expense projections on past performance where possible.

- Consider new trends and market factors.

Table 8.2 Summary Marketing Expense Budget								
Marketing Expense	**Jan**	**Feb**	**Mar**	**1st Qtr**	**Apr**	**May**	**Jun**	**2nd Qtr**
Direct Mail								
Recruitment								
Retention								
Advertising								
Print								
Online								
Trade Show								
Annual meeting								
Industry show								
Catalog								
Fall								
Spring								
Total expense								
Projected revenue								

- Prioritize spending to match the priority of marketing strategies.

- Document how you arrived at expense budgets so you remember the logic of your projections and can explain it.

- Plan to review the budget forecast to actual spending regularly (at least quarterly) and adjust spending and forecasts as appropriate.

- Keep a copy of your original budget projections; it'll come in handy during budget reviews.

Once you arrive at a number, ask yourself if it's realistic. It's common to revise revenue and expense estimates more than once before settling on a final budget, in part because indirect costs (overhead) will be factored in to compile the overall organization budget. Do the best you can to reflect what you expect will happen in the next twelve months.

Format

Utilize your association's spreadsheet software or forms to submit your budget. A sample summary marketing expense budget is shown in Table 8.2.

Chapter 9

Define Controls
and Measurements

*The professional's grasp of the numbers is a measure of the control
s/he has over the events that the figures represent.*

—Judge Harold S. Geneen

A good marketing plan isn't proven effective until it's implemented and measured. *Marketing controls* are methods to measure and evaluate marketing plans, adjusting as needed to achieve the objectives. Your marketing controls should inform you about what is occurring and why it's occurring, as well as indicate where corrective action is necessary—or at least provide some clues to investigate.

You'll need to monitor the effectiveness and profitability of all strategies continuously and implement corrective action if results fall short of objectives. Ideally, marketing controls will report marketing results monthly, quarterly, and annually, allowing you to discern whether results indicate a normal trend or potential gap that requires adjustment.

Typical controls monitor sales results, market share, customer satisfaction, profitability, and effectiveness of communication channels as well as other objectives defined in the marketing plan—often by product or service, market segment, and other variables important to your association. These controls help you determine whether to increase or decrease resources for specific products or services and marketing tactics.

The true test of an effective marketing control is whether it delivers the information you need for marketing decision making. Your association should already generate key reports to compare results to objectives. The usefulness of the information often depends on your association's database software and the marketing acumen of the person who crafted the marketing department's informational needs when the software was purchased.

Many associations struggle with antiquated database technology, leaving significant information gaps. If you're faced with information gaps, be sure to include these needs under *resource requirements* in your marketing plan. While your reports may not look exactly like the examples shown here, at a minimum they should communicate the same data points.

The following are helpful tools to monitor your marketing plan: a source code registry, a sales results to objective report, direct mail analysis, and response rate analysis.

Source Code Registry

A *source code* is a symbol, usually alphabetic or numeric, applied to every marketing collateral and communication vehicle to measure actual sales resulting from each form and type of communication. Ever placed a catalog order by phone and had the customer service representative ask you for "the code printed next to your name on the back cover"? That's the source code. The company is measuring the effectiveness of the catalog by tracking sales generated and comparing results to other marketing communications such as display ads or its Web site. So should you. Over time this tells you which marketing communications work more effectively with your target audiences.

While simple, a system of source coding all marketing communications is mandatory for effective control of a marketing plan. Without it you're missing vital information for sound marketing decision making (and are likely wasting money).

Format

A simple way to track source codes is to create a source code registry or master list that compiles all the relevant information about all marketing communications (see Table 9.1). This information will be used by your information technology department to program codes into the database, by your customer service department to collect and enter codes on all customer orders, and by your operations department to fulfill customer orders.

Table 9.1	Source Code Registry				
Source Code	Communication Tactic	Date (Month & Year)	Headline	Market Segment or Prospect List	Special Offers
1000	**Direct mail**				
1001	No.10 package: membership*	Feb '02	Enroll Today!	Prospect list 1	Enroll now, save $20
1002	Product catalog: spring	Apr '03	Great Stuff for You	Members Prospect list 2 Prospect list 3	Buy $100, free shipping
1003	Self mailer: affinity MasterCard	Jun '03	Exclusively for My Members	Members	0% for first 6 months
1004					
2000	**Events**				
2001	Exhibit: our bookstore	Sep '03	Save 10%	Annual meeting attendees	Buy at show, save 10%
2002					
2003					

Table 9.1 (*continued* on the following page)

*Mailing uses a # 10 business envelope.

Table 9.1 *(continued* from the previous page)

Source Code	Communication Tactic	Date (Month & Year)	Headline	Market Segment or Prospect List	Special Offers
3000	**Telemarketing**				
3001					
3002					
3003					
4000	**Advertising**				
4001A	Magazine: XYZ trade journal	Jun '03	We're Cool! Join Today!	XYZ members XYZ subscribers	
4001B	Magazine: XYZ trade journal	Jul '03	We're Cool! Join Today!	XYZ members XYZ subscribers	
4001C	Magazine: XYZ trade journal	Aug '03	We're Cool! Join Today!	XYZ members XYZ subscribers	
4002	Web banner: www.pdq.com	Jan– June '04	We're Cool! Join Today!	PDQ site visitors	
4003					
4004					

Sales Results to Objective Report

Most likely, your finance department monitors sales results to objective for the association—at least in sum. While financial reports typically show actual sales results and the variance to sales forecasts, often what's missing is a breakdown by individual product or service, by customer segment, and by communication tactic. This information is essential to make cost-effective product development and promotion decisions.

Format. See Tables 9.2 and 9.3.

Table 9.2	Sales Results to Objective by Market Segment and Product or Service				
By Month, Quarter & Year	**Target Audience 1**	**Target Audience 2**	**Target Audience 3**	**Total Customers**	**% Sales $**
Product/ Service 1					
Unit forecast	150	100	50	300	
Unit actual	142	104	69	315	
Variance (+/−)	−8	4	19	15	
% of forecast	−5%	4%	38%	5%	
Sales forecast	$33,750	$22,500	$11,250	$67,500	
Actual sales	$31,950	$23,400	$15,525	$70,875	39%
Variance (+/−)	$(1,800)	$900	$4,275	$3,375	
% of forecast	−5%	4%	38%	5%	
Product/ Service 2					
Unit forecast	250	300	250	800	
Unit actual	114	234	241	589	
Variance (+/−)	−136	−66	−9	−211	
% of forecast	−54%	−22%	−4%	−26%	
Sales forecast	$37,500	$45,000	$37,500	$120,000	
Actual sales	$15,390	$31,590	$32,535	$79,515	43%
Variance (+/−)	$(22,110)	$(13,410)	$(4,965)	$(40,485)	
% of forecast	−59%	−30%	−13%	−34%	
Product/ Service 3					
Unit forecast	75	100	125	300	
Unit actual	150	139	162	451	

Table 9.2 (*continued* on the following page)

Table 9.2   (*continued* from the previous page)

By Month, Quarter & Year	Target Audience 1	Target Audience 2	Target Audience 3	Total Customers	% Sales $
Variance (+/−)	75	39	37	151	
% of forecast	100%	39%	30%	50%	
Sales forecast	$6,000	$8,000	$10,000	$24,000	
Actual sales	$10,800	$10,008	$11,664	$32,472	18%
Variance (+/−)	$4,800	$2,008	$1,664	$8,472	
% of forecast	80%	25%	17%	35%	
Total unit forecast	475	500	425	1,400	
Total unit actual	406	477	472	1,355	
Variance (+/−)	(69)	(23)	47	(45)	
% of forecast	−15%	−5%	11%	−3%	
Total sales forecast	$77,250	$75,500	$58,750	$211,500	
Total sales actual	$58,140	$64,998	$59,724	$182,862	
Variance (+/−)	$(19,110)	$(10,502)	$974	$(28,638)	
% of forecast	−25%	−14%	2%	−14%	

Assumptions:

Product 1: Forecast average sales price (ASP) = $225; actual ASP = $225.
Product 2: Forecast ASP = $150; actual ASP = $135, due to returns and refunds.
Product 3: Forecast ASP = $80; actual ASP = $72, due to 10% discount on all sales.

Table 9.3	Sales Results to Objective by Marketing Communication Tactic												
Tactic	Source Code	Month 1			Month 2			Month 3			Total Quarter		
		Sales	Expense	Net Sales	Sales	Expense	Net Sales	Sales	Expense	Net Sales	Sales	Expense	Net Sales $
Direct Mail													
Mail 1	1001	$3,600	$6,425	$(2,825)	$4,050	$-0-	$4,050	$2,250	$-0-	$2,250	$9,900	$6,425	$3,475
Mail 2	1002	6,824	4,893	1,931	5,250	-0-	5,250	3,960	-0-	3,960	16,034	4,893	$11,141
Mail 3	1003	4,230	3,400	830	3,500	-0-	3,500	3,200	-0-	3,200	10,930	3,400	$7,530
Total Direct mail		$14,654	$14,718	$(64)	$12,800	$-0-	$12,800	$9,410	$-0-	$9,410	$36,864	$14,718	$22,146
Advertising													
Publication 1	4001A	$-0-	$1,250	$(1,250)	$360	$1,250	$(890)	$450	$1,250	$(800)	$810	3,750	$(2,940)
	4001B	$ -0-	1,250	(1,250)	450	1,250	(800)	990	1,250	(260)	1,440	3,750	$(2,310)
	4001C	90	1,250	(1,160)	630	1,250	(620)	1,980	1,250	730	2,700	3,750	$1,050
Publication 2													
Publication 3													
Total advertising													

Table 9.3 (*continued* on the following page)

Table 9.3   (*continued* from the previous page)

Tactic	Source Code	Month 1			Month 2			Month 3			Total Quarter		
		Sales	Expense	Net Sales	Sales	Expense	Net Sales	Sales	Expense	Net Sales	Sales	Expense	Net Sales $
Events													
Event 1													
Event 2													
Event 3													
Event 4													
Event 5													
Total Events													
Tele-marketing													
Campaign 1													
Campaign 2													
Total Tele-marketing													
Grand Total													

Direct Mail Break-even Analysis

Direct mail is a common form of promotion for associations. A good way to plan and measure direct mail campaigns is to calculate a simple break-even or response rate analysis. A Direct Mail Break-even Analysis (Table 9.4) calculates the number of product or service unit sales needed to cover direct expenses for each campaign.

Formula

Step 1. Identify and add all expenses associated with your direct mail campaign, as well as the per unit purchase price.

Table 9.4 Direct Mail Break-even Analysis		
Activity	**Direct Mail Expense**	**Calculation**
List rental (5000 names)	$425	= No. of names rented ÷ 1000 × Cost per thousand
Copywriting	1,500	
Graphic design	1,000	
Printing	1,250	
Mail shop	750	
Postage	<u>1,500</u>	
Total Direct Mail expense	<u>$6,425</u>	
Sales Price Per Unit	$90	
Break-even Points		
Units	72	= Total fixed costs ÷ sales price per unit (rounded up)
Revenue	$6,515	= Break-even units x sales price per unit
Response rate	1.45%	= Break-even units ÷ total mail pieces

Note: Assumption is made that product shipping is pass-through, at customer expense.

Step 2. To determine the number of break-even units you must sell to cover expenses, divide total expenses by the per unit sales price. Be sure to round up (or automatically add 1).

Step 3. Next, multiply the number of break-even units by the per unit sales price. This confirms how much revenue will be derived. Be sure this number is higher than direct mail expenses.

Step 4. Divide the number of break-even units by the total number of mail pieces dropped. This determines the average response rate you will need to break even. Standard direct mail response rates will vary depending on campaign variables. As a standard rule of thumb, expect a 1 to 3 percent rate of response.

Direct Mail Response Rate Analysis

A *response rate analysis* determines the response rate at which you begin to earn profits.

Formula

Step 1. Indicate your assumptions, including total number of mail pieces, sales price per unit, and average response rates from 0.5 to 4 percent.

Step 2. To determine projected sales volume, multiply the response rate percentage by the total number of mail pieces. To determine projected sales revenue, multiply the projected sales volume by the sales price per unit.

Step 3. Subtract the total direct mail expense (calculated in your direct mail break-even analysis) from the projected sales revenue to determine projected net sales revenue. The point at which the projected net sales revenue is a positive number is the response rate you'll need to break even. (In Table 9.5, that's 75 units.)

Format

In this section of the plan, it's enough to present a brief narrative description of each marketing control, including frequency, along with a sample of the related report. This then becomes the structure for reporting the progress of your marketing plan.

Table 9.5 Direct Mail Response Rate Analysis							
Assumptions							
Total mail pieces	5000	5000	5000	5000	5000	5000	5000
Sales price per unit	$90	$90	$90	$90	$90	$90	$90
Response rate	0.50%	1%	1.50%	2%	2.50%	3%	4%
Projections							
Sales volume	25	50	75	100	125	150	200
Sales revenue	$2,250	$4,500	$6,750	$9,000	$11,250	$13,500	$18,000
Total Direct Mail Expense	$6,425	$6,425	$6,425	$6,425	$6,425	$6,425	$6,425
Projected Net Sales Revenue	$(4,175)	$(1,925)	$325	$2,575	$4,825	$7,075	$11,575

Chapter 10

Write the Executive Summary

The world is round and the place, which may seem like the end, may also be only the beginning.

—Ivy Baker, Actress

Essentially, the executive summary equates to the Cliffs Notes for your marketing plan. This section communicates the main plot and key characters in a simple, direct fashion that's easy to read. It is not a sales presentation to persuade the reader to accept your point of view. Rather, the executive summary provides a context for the plan and organizes essential information in the reader's mind (see Table 10.1).

A formal presentation of the marketing plan to colleagues is an important internal communication practice that will also help you refine the executive summary. Once you've completed the plan, develop a slide presentation and script. Think about how you will walk colleagues through the content highlights. This will add clarity to your executive summary and ultimately aid colleagues' understanding and acceptance of the marketing plan.

Formula

Journalists use a simple formula to construct a lead for a news story. The who, what, when, where, why, and how of the story are summarized in the first few lines, with more cogent details elaborated upon as the story continues. Use the same formula for the executive summary of your marketing plan.

Craft your executive summary as though you're telling a story. Answer these questions:

- What is the story about?
- Who are the main characters in the story?
- When does the story occur?
- Where does the action take place?
- Why is the story important and unique?
- How does the plot unfold?

Format

While a marketing plan always opens with an executive summary, it's the last section of the plan you'll actually write. It may be a few paragraphs or a few pages, depending on the nature and complexity of the marketing plan.

Writing the executive summary requires keen discernment on your part. To capture and frame the reader's attention, you need to include the most compelling information in a clear, concise manner. For example, it's more important to state a fact than to substantiate it (which can always be accomplished with cross-references).

The executive summary is your one chance for a good first impression. Make the most of it!

Table 10.1   Anatomy of an Executive Summary

Question	Answer
What . . . is the story about?	*Once upon a time* (in the next twelve months), *we* (association) *aim to achieve certain goals* (business and marketing objectives) *by using multiple techniques* (strategies) *in particular ways* (positioning). *This is a challenge because* (weaknesses, threats) *but we'll compensate with* (strengths, opportunities). *To get to the goal we'll make stuff* (products/ services) *that several people* (customers) *in certain places* (market environment) *want and can afford* (cost). *We'll send the stuff to many access points* (convenience) *and then tell everybody about it* (communication).
Who . . . are the main characters in the story?	Customers, prospects Competitors Marketing channels, suppliers Strategic partners, allies Staff
When . . . does the story occur?	Timing
Where . . . does the action take place?	Overview of market situation, emphasis on market dynamics and trends
Why . . . is our story important and unique?	Overview of association situation, emphasis on strengths and opportunities Positioning, emphasis on competitive advantage Financial forecast(s)
How . . . does the plot unfold?	Brief summary of products and services Highlights of key strategies, resource requirements, controls and measurements

Appendix 1

ASAE Association Marketing Core Competencies

The ASAE Marketing Section Council identified the following key skills and knowledge necessary for association marketers to succeed.

1. **Marketing planning:** market segmentation; forecasting; SWOT analysis (strengths, weaknesses, opportunities, and threats); market share analysis; and articulation of customer, cost, convenience, and communication.

2. **Market research:** analysis and interpretation; management of qualitative and quantitative information; competitive intelligence; research instrument design; consumer buying behavior models; and application of market research to marketing planning.

3. **Customer strategy:** one-to-one relationship marketing; lifetime value; database management; database marketing; and customer relationship management.

4. **Product and service strategy:** product and service development; product life cycles; and branding.

5. **Distribution strategy:** endorsements and affinity; partnerships and alliances; sales management; fulfillment operations; Internet and e-commerce; and inventory and production management.

6. **Pricing strategy:** cost measurement; strategies and techniques; budgeting and financial management; elastic and inelastic market analysis; and nondues revenue and royalties.

7. **Marketing communications:** concept development; branding; campaign strategy; copywriting; graphic design; list management (prospects, customers); marketing tactics (traditional and online); results measurement and analysis; and member-to-member communications.

8. **Business management:** association management principles; ethics; strategic planning; human resources and outsourcing relationship management; negotiation and consensus building; project management; team building; marketing management; legal issues; and technology applications.

Daily Marketing Action Plan

My Association (Fiscal Year) Daily Marketing Action Plan			
	By When	**Who**	**Done √**
Strategy 1: Brief Descriptive Phrase (Association goal this strategy supports)		**Team leader or manager**	
Tactic 1: Briefly outline highlights of tactical plan here.			
Actions: Description of specific action required.	Month/Day	Person responsible	
	By When	**Who**	**Done √**
Strategy 2: Brief Descriptive Phrase (Association goal this strategy supports)		**Team leader or manager**	
Tactic 1: Briefly outline highlights of tactical plan here.			
Actions: Description of specific action required.	Month/Day	Person responsible	
Tactic 2: Briefly outline highlights of tactical plan here.			
Actions: Description of specific action required.	Month/Day	Person responsible	

Appendix 3

Direct Mail Project Timeline

Team	Week 1	Week 2	Week 3	Week 4	Week 5	Week 6
Marketer	Set parameters Get product information	Craft offer Concept meeting	Requests for quotations Final copy	Select vendors Prepare purchase orders	Order list	Proof routed in-house
Designer		Concept meeting		Preliminary design	Preliminary design presentation	Proof to USPS*
Printer		Concept meeting		Submit quote	Schedule press	Order supplies
Mailer		Concept meeting		Submit quote	Schedule job	Order supplies
	Week 7	**Week 8**	**Week 9**	**Week 10**	**Week 11**	**Week 12**
Marketer	Approve final proof	Approve blueline	Extra week for breakdowns	Approve address proof	Postage check cut/deposited	Alert Ops
Designer	Edits final proof	Disk to printer Approve blueline	Extra week for breakdowns			
Printer		Pre-press blueline	Printing	Printing	Extra week for breakdowns	
Mailer		Lists to mailer	Data processing	Address proof	Extra week for breakdowns	Mail process and drop

*Your customer service representative at the U.S. Postal Service should inspect the proof to make sure the mailing piece (if self-mailer) or envelope conforms to postal regulations for your mailing class.

Glossary

Advantages: Factors that distinguish what is unique or special about the features of a product or service.

Average sales price (ASP): The average dollar cost to the customer per unit of a product or service.

Benefits: Favorable or desired experiences the customer derives when purchasing or using a product or service.

Behaviorals: Qualitative information that provides insights about a customer's relationship to a specific type of product, service, or brand, including desired benefits, usage, loyalty, and readiness to buy.

Competitive analysis: An examination and reporting of a range of information about your competitors in contrast to your organization.

Contribution margin: Percentage ratio of "true" profit for each sales dollar. Also known as *net profit margin* or *net margin*.

> *Calculation:* Net Sales Revenue – Total Variable Costs (COGS, sales commissions, marketing expenses) ÷ Net Sales Revenue = Contribution Margin.

Cost of sales: Includes costs to the association, such as merchandise purchase, production and/or freight, necessary to make products or services available for sale. Also known as *cost of goods sold (COGS)*.

Demand: The volume or extent of a market whose customers (individuals or organizations) are ready and able to buy a product or service at a certain price. Often available via secondary market research data.

> *Calculation for unit volume:* Total Number of Product or Service Units Sold by Each Competitor in a Market Added Together = Unit Volume of Market Demand.

> *Calculation for dollar value:* Total Number of Product or Service Units Sold by Each Competitor multiplied by Average Sales Price of Each Competitor = Dollar Value of Market Demand By Each Competitor. Add the Dollar Value of All Competitors Together = Dollar Value of Market Demand.

Demographics: Customer information that distinguishes a range of physical, social, and economic attributes such as age, gender, income level, marital status, and ethnic origin.

Elasticity: Customers' degree of sensitivity to price and their resulting demand for a product or service. High elasticity means there is an increased market demand when price changes; low elasticity means there is no change in market demand when price changes.

Features: Factual attributes or characteristics of a product or service expressed in terms of form or function.

Geographics: Customer information that identifies physical location, such as country, state, region, and local area.

Gross margin: A percentage ratio that measures your ability to simultaneously control costs, sustain or increase sales, and sustain or increase sales prices. Also known as *gross profit margin*.

Calculation: Gross Profit ÷ Net Sales Revenue = Percentage of Gross Margin

Gross profit: The total dollars remaining after sales and operating costs are deducted from sales revenue. Also known as *net revenue on sales*.

Calculation: Net Sales Revenue − Cost of Sales = Gross Profit

Gross sales revenue: The total dollars generated from total number of units sold in a specific time period.

Gross sales volume: The total number of units sold in a specific period of time, such as number of annual memberships, event registrations or publication subscriptions.

Market: The sum of all customers and potential customers, whether individuals or organizations, who want *or* need *and* can afford your products or services.

Market advantage: The primary benefits that satisfy customer wants or needs more effectively than a competitor's.

Market dynamics: The uncontrollable external demographic, economic, natural, cultural, technological, political, and legal variables affecting a market, which in some way impacts your association's sales.

Market forecast: An educated prediction of total anticipated customers and sales by segment, anticipated growth rate, and other variables for an entire market, based on an analysis of prevailing market dynamics.

Market growth rate: The degree by which a market is increasing or decreasing in size, expressed as a percentage per year in dollar value or unit volume. Also known as *compound annual growth rate (CAGR)*.

Calculation for Dollar Value: Dollar Value of the Most Recent Year Total Market Sales minus the Dollar Value of Immediate Prior Year Total Market Sales divided by Dollar Value of Immediate Prior Year multiplied by 100 = % Market Growth Rate

Calculation for Unit Volume: Total Number of Units Sold in Most Recent Year minus the Total Number of Units Sold in Immediate Prior Year ÷ Total Number of Units Sold in Immediate Prior Year multiplied by 100 = % Market Growth Rate.

Percentage Increase = Most Recent Year > Immediate Prior Year (+ %)

Percentage Decrease = Most Recent Year < Immediate Prior Year (− %)

Market research: The collection, analysis, interpretation, and reporting of quantitative and qualitative information for marketing decision making.

Primary market research: Information collected and published by your organization, either in house or by a research firm.

Secondary market research: Information collected and published by outside organizations, such as industry experts, government agencies, academic institutions, associations, and the media.

Market segment: A subset of the market with like characteristics whose wants, needs, and purchasing habits are similar.

Market segmentation: The practice of dividing a market into smaller groups sharing similar characteristics.

Market share: The percentage of a market that currently buys a specific product or service from your organization compared to the percentage of the market that buys from other competitors. Expressed as a percentage of the total number of customers in a market, and a percentage of the dollar value of total sales for a market. Also known as *market penetration*.

Market trends: Previous and anticipated tendencies in relation to the current market situation.

Market universe: The totality of a market expressed in size or dollar value of sales (*i.e.*, all customers and potential customers who want *or* need *and*

can afford your products or services *and* are expected to buy). Also known as *market potential.*

Marketing controls: Methods used to measure and evaluate marketing plans, adjusting as needed to achieve the objectives.

Net sales revenue: The total dollar value of all product or service sales, after returns and refunds.

Calculation: Gross Sales Revenue minus the xDollar Value of Product or Service Returns and Refunds = Net Sales Revenue

Net sales volume: The total number of product or service units sold, after returns and refunds.

Calculation: Gross Sales Volume minus the Number of Product or Service Returns or Refunds = Net Sales Volume

Positioning: An articulation of the most sustainable benefit(s) that gives the greatest leverage for the organization and its products or services and that cannot be owned by any competitor.

Price: The amount of money you ask the customer to pay for products and services.

Psychographics: Customer information that defines attitudes, beliefs, opinions, personalities, and lifestyles.

Sales forecast: Predicts total anticipated sales and related revenue by market segment for a specific period of time, typically one year.

Situation analysis: An examination and reporting of the significant circumstances and conditions of your internal and external environments so as to understand their nature, proportion, function, and interrelationship.

Strategies: The logic used to position the association in the market and achieve the business and marketing objectives, given the situation analysis.

Supply: The amount of a product or service type available in a market for purchase at a given price. Often available via secondary research data.

Calculation for unit volume: Total Number of Product or Service Units Produced by Each Competitor in a Market Added Together = Unit Volume of Market Supply

Calculation for dollar value: Total Number of Product or Service Units Produced by Each Competitor multiplied by Average Sales Price of Each Competitor = Dollar Value of Market Supply by Each Competitor

Add the Dollar Value of All Competitors Together = Dollar Value of Market Supply

SWOT analysis: An examination and reporting of an organization's strengths (S), weaknesses (W), opportunities (O), and threats (T), particularly in relation to the competitive market environment.

Tactics: Specific marketing initiatives, methods, and actions employed to implement a strategy.

Target audience: The specific market segments you identify as the most likely customers for your products or services. Target audiences are characteristically identifiable (size and scope can be defined and measured); accessible (can be reached via your marketing channels); serviceable (your association possesses the resources to adequately serve the size and nature of the target audience); and profitable (large enough with enough buying power for you to pursue).

Unique selling proposition (USP): An articulation of the primary feature, advantage, or benefit of a product or service that directly fulfills your target audiences' wants or needs and that distinguishes it from competitive products or services.